Some people were no†

'Like everything else Tom writes, *A*
to read, relevant, accessible, and
remind you why the good news of Jesus read,
Chris Morphew – *Author of* Best News Ever *and the* Big Questions *series*

'The Bible is the bestselling, most widely distributed, and most read book in the history of the world. But what can a book from 2000 years ago possibly have in common with me today? Tom French's *A Dozen Disappointing Disciples* shows us that we have way more in common with the twelve bumbling, foolhardy, and headstrong disciples of Jesus than we dared imagine. By reading this book, we will find that their shortcomings are also our shortcomings. But more importantly, we will see that their path of redemption is the same one that we can take today.'
Sam Chan – *City Bible Forum, Australia and Author of* Evangelism in a Skeptical World, How to Talk About Jesus (Without Being That Guy), *and* Topical Preaching in a Complex World

'Do you ever feel disappointed with your own efforts? Do you worry about disappointing God? Tom French wants you to meet Peter, James, John, Thomas, and the other disciples - and mostly, he wants you to meet Jesus, who has as much patience, generosity, and life-changing grace for you as he did for them.
Drawing a line between the Gospel stories and our own everyday lives is a challenging art, but Tom makes it look effortless. This encounter with Jesus and his disciples will puncture your ego, lay your fears to rest, help you think about stuff in new ways, and offer you a mission in life. Also, it's really funny!'
Dr Natasha Moore – *Author of* For the Love of God *and winner of the 2020 Australian Christian Book of the Year award*

'*A Dozen Disappointing Disciples* is full of Tom's quirky humour and funny stories that are well pitched for teenagers. But the real genius in this book is the way Tom communicates profound biblical and theological insights with such understated simplicity. The book not only engages with the Bible but is also full of excellent historical information on the New Testament background. This book will both serve teenagers in following Jesus with his disciples and deepen our understanding of how to read and teach the New Testament for leaders.'
Mike Dicker – *Principal, Youthworks College Sydney*

'Because it's Tom, you know this is going to be a fun read that points you to Jesus while positively relying upon the Holy Spirit to change the world. This is a timely book for a season where many of us feel like we can't do anything unless we are famous or superhuman. Tom makes it clear that God can use you; just look at the disciples. Let's rejoin with Jesus to change the world with His gospel.'
Matt Gelding – *Director, Soul Survivor Australia*

A DOZEN DISAPPOINTING DISCIPLES

How to Do Stupid Stuff and Still Change the World

TOM FRENCH

FRENDRUSSI PRESS

A DOZEN DISAPPOINTING DISCIPLES: HOW TO DO STUPID STUFF
AND STILL CHANGE THE WORLD

ISBN 978-0-6483041-8-0
Ebook ISBN 978-0-6483041-9-7

First published 2021 by Frendrussi Press
Melbourne, VIC, Australia

Cover illustration by Matt Baker
Cover design by Emily Sandrussi

For Mum and Dad

Two excellent disciples who have discipled me
excellently

CONTENTS

ACKNOWLEDGEMENTS

I don't quite know where to mark the momentous life events that have happened while writing this book, so I feel this is a good place to acknowledge them. This is the acknowledgements, after all. On a personal scale, some time while I was nearing the end of the first draft, my daughter Layla was conceived (I have no idea how that happened), and somewhere in the process of receiving people's comments on the second draft, she was born. (Turns out it's a lot quicker to grow a kid than make a book – and easier on my part too!) Now I've been finishing up the edits while she sleeps on me, or plays beside me, while Emily helps me carve out space to get this done. Layla has turned our life upside down in the best possible way.

Meanwhile, as I was plugging away at the book in late 2019, Australia was experiencing one of the worst bushfire seasons on record. Thanks, climate change! It was sad and stressful. For us, it mucked up our holiday plans but for many others it was so much more terrible. As those months of fires came to a close, along came the Covid-19 pandemic. On top of the initial national lockdown, Melbourne, where we live, spent sixteen weeks in a hard lockdown, which wasn't great for my mental health but was excellent for getting books finished. However, I know we have suffered little compared to much of the rest of the world.

As I write this in June 2021 we're in our fourth lockdown. A few months ago we moved apartments; now we have a view of a beautiful park instead of a concrete wall and motorway, so it's an easier way to be under house arrest. I know the world is going to be different when all this is over, but I don't know how. I feel like I've written a book for an unknown future, which I guess is the case with all books, but everything feels extra malleable at the moment. I'm just relying on the fact that a lot of the stuff the disciples did will always be objectively daft, no matter what kind of apocalyptic wasteland or pandemic-free, climate-change-fixed paradise we inhabit.

Okay, that's enough epoch documentation, I should get on with all the rest of the acknowledgements.

To begin, I acknowledge the Traditional Custodians of the land on which the majority of this book was created, the Wurundjeri people of the Kulin nation. I pay my respects to their Elders past, present, and future.

It takes a lot of people to make a good book. I guess I could have done it all myself, but it'd be a sad, self-published mess rather than this much more polished, self-published extravaganza.

Pretty much the whole time I have been writing this book, I have been the youth minister at Inner North Youth Group. The youth and the leaders are an excellent bunch of young (and young-ish) people who I love hanging out with, even if sometimes it has to be on Zoom.

I'm also very thankful for my church, Merri Creek Anglican, and my boss, Peter Carolane. I love all the support, and meals, we've got from our church over the past few months. What a great community we have.

A significant group of people who have made this book much better are all those who took the time to read it (or some of it) and give feedback, whether that's one line or an essay. Those people are Amy Brown, John Buckley, James Delanty, Emily Hayes, Anthea McCall, Johnny Sharpe, and Karen Winsemius. Your expert opinions have been so helpful in making this book much smarter, more sensitive, and wiser than it otherwise would have been.

Very special thanks goes to the teenage reader crew, William Denholm, Claudie Miller, and Liz Sonneman. I'm so glad you took the time to read and let me know what you think. You've improved this book with your excellent insights, and you also made me get rid of some of my least good jokes. All future readers thank you!

Chris Morphew, thanks for live messaging me your book reading and being a constantly great champion of my books. Now that I've got this book sorted, I can get back to editing season two of *Questions You're Not Asking*.

Thanks to Howie, for all your backhanded support. Especially for that time I was planting a church and you said on Facebook, 'I don't think we need more churches, but if we did, you should go to Tom's.'

Thanks to Joshua Kuswadi. You used your majestic research skills to find and correct the Philip Yancey quote from Chapter 14 for me in an actual book when all I had was Google Books and my audiobook (neither of which have page numbers). May this acknowledgement be a fitting reward for your extraordinary service.

Graham Stanton, as always I'm thankful for your coaching, support, and friendship.

Jo Stockdale, I reckon we're getting pretty good at this editing thing. Thanks for taking the time to make sure my book is as close to being a real book as it can be and for putting up with all my silly jokes. It's consistently great working with you!

Gina Denholm, once again, you've done an excellent job finding all my missing words, comma splices, and typesetting mistakes. I hope this one hasn't been too full of issues.

Matt Baker, you've created some excellent art for the cover. Thank you. Your talent continues to amaze me!

For my wonderful family – Hannah, Jo, Victor, Sebastian, Hugo, Steve, Valentina, and Oscar. Thanks for all your support and love. I haven't seen much of you all lately but I still love having you all in my life, and I love how much you love Emily, Layla, and me.

Jane and John, Mum and Dad, you're the best! Thanks for reading this and telling me all your thoughts and improving this book so much. But more than that, thanks for always loving me, encouraging me, and introducing me to Jesus. I hope I'm an okay son.

Layla, it's so great to have you around. Thanks for keeping me company, for smiling at me for no reason, and for being the cutest baby in the world. I hope you read this one day and know that we've loved you from even before we met you.

Emily, excellent wife, wonderful mother, best friend. Thanks for all your continued love, encouragement, and grace. I still love you like the mountains.

Once again, as always, all praise and thanks goes to God – Father, Son, and Holy Spirit. I'm so glad you've called and saved this disappointing disciple, who you are somehow not disappointed in. All glory to you!

INTRODUCTION

I have a problem with Jesus.

That's possibly not the correct way to start a Christian book, but I'm just telling you the truth.

Here is my issue. As a Christian, I regularly hear about how I have to be more like Jesus. I listen to talks, I read books, I sing songs – all of them are about being like Jesus. The problem is, well, Jesus. Have you met the guy? He's amazing. He's perfect. He is literally a god. He *is* God. How can I possibly be like him?

If someone said to me, 'Be like Dwayne "The Rock" Johnson', I'd respond, 'No. You be like Dwayne "The Rock" Johnson'. I don't want to get up at four o'clock every morning and work out in the Iron Paradise, eat massive amounts of protein, run a bunch of companies, produce films, act in films, make time for my fans, and find time to see my family. That's too much work. Some of those things by themselves would be good. I wouldn't mind committing to making films or working out more, but all of those things together? No way. I couldn't. Happily, no one is expecting me to be like The Rock. It's absurd. If you've seen me, you'll know it's absurd.

So, if I can't be like Dwayne, then how can I ever hope to be like Jesus? I'm not sure about Jesus' workout routine, but in every other way, Jesus blows everyone else out of the water. When we read the stories of his life, we see he was kind, loving, gentle, smart, wise, funny, brilliant, passionate, friendly, fierce, and probably a rather good tradesman to boot. He is the perfect human. So as much as I like Jesus (and I really, really like Jesus), sometimes I find it difficult to imagine that I could be like him. I'm not even good with a hammer.

Jesus was a brilliant teacher; sometimes when I do Bible talks, I accidentally say 'Satan' when I mean to say 'Jesus'.

Jesus healed the sick; I can't even fix a bike tyre.

Jesus stood up to the religious authorities; I have trouble standing up to Siri.

Jesus rose from the dead; I struggle to get up to my alarm.

Jesus was without sin; I am definitely not that.

I cannot be like Jesus.

But I'll tell you who I can be like – the disciples. Jesus' twelve buddies. Now, there is a biblical example I can get behind. They were proud, scared, thick, doubtful, jealous, angry, weird, dishonest, faithless, and so much more! That sounds much more like me. When I read the biographies of Jesus (the books of the Bible known as the Gospels – Mathew, Mark, Luke, and John), I admire Jesus, but I identify with the disciples.

These were the guys who didn't understand Jesus' teaching, even when he was speaking plainly. They fought amongst themselves and they fought with others. They were racists, terrorists, traitors, and liars. They had good intentions that went quite wrong. They had bad intentions that also went wrong.

This book, as is obvious from the title, is about the disciples. Here is what's so amazing about the disciples: even though they were so flawed and seem pretty disappointing, they ended up changing the world. Their faltering following of Jesus led to the shaping of the world as we know it today. And if God can change the world through them, he can change the world through you and me too. That's good news.

So, I'll tell you what we're going to do in this book. We will look at the stories of the disciples. Particularly, we're going to focus on those times they did or said something stupid. Seeing as each of the chapters is based on a passage in the Bible, you would do well to read the passage in your Bible (or on your app) before you read the chapter. Also, you can read this book cover to cover, or drop in on the chapters that seem most interesting. But if you do just read a few chapters, I reckon it'd be worth at least reading the final one and the conclusion to see what happens in the end.

Who were the disciples?

Now, before we get into the stories of the disciples, it might be worth knowing who they are. The problem is, while we know a lot about a few of the disciples, and a small amount about some of them, we know next to nothing about the rest of them. However, I'll tell you what we know, and we'll trust God that the rest won't be covered in the exam.

This is what Mark 3:13–15 tells us about when Jesus chose the twelve disciples: 'Jesus went up on a mountainside and called to him those he wanted, and they came to him. He appointed twelve that they might be with him and that he might send them out to preach and to have authority to drive out demons.'

This moment comes a little way into Jesus' ministry. He'd already done a bunch of travelling around the countryside, healing people, casting out demons, and doing his impressive teaching. Because of this, he had a load of women and men following him, travelling around with him, and listening to his teaching. Throughout Jesus' ministry he had many disciples. However, Jesus chose to call a particular group of twelve to play a special role. When I talk about the disciples in this book, unless I say otherwise, I'm talking about the group known as 'the Twelve'.

Why did he call twelve? The number twelve was very significant to the Jewish people of Jesus' day. This was because ancient Israelite football teams had twelve players, and football was very popular at the time. Obviously, Jesus wanted to compete in the local leagues. They called themselves the Nazareth Nazguls.

That last paragraph is fake news. I have no idea how many players were on an Israelite football team in AD 26. The number twelve was important for a much more significant reason. Ancient Israel, the descendants of Abraham, called by God to be his chosen people, a light to the nations and a blessing to the world, comprised twelve tribes. Each tribe was named after their patriarch, one of the twelve sons of Jacob from whom they were descended (Genesis 35:22–26). Unfortunately, they hadn't lived up to their calling. After repeatedly falling into sin, idolatry, and rebellion against God over a couple of hundred years, foreign powers took all of Israel into captivity and away from their homeland. When these foreign powers were defeated by other nations, only two tribes of Israel came back. The other ten had been scattered across the known world. They intermarried with other people groups and lost their identity as the people of God. (Some, as we'll discuss later, did hang around Israel, but they inter-married with other local people groups and became the Samaritans.)[1]

Around five hundred years later, Jesus called twelve disciples to himself. He was signifying that he was beginning a new Israel. Where previously the people of God had not lived up to their calling, now Jesus was doing a new thing. This new Israel would bring the blessing of God to all the world, just as old Israel was meant to do.

The role of these disciples was to 'preach and... drive out demons'. While this may sound like some kind of evangelical Ghostbusters (which I can imagine as a badly made Christian movie on PureFlix), essentially what it means is that their ministry was to be an extension of

---

1. I just gave you a very brief history of the nation of Israel before Jesus. If you read the Old Testament you'll get a much more comprehensive picture of what went on.

Jesus' ministry. The work of the disciples was not just to follow Jesus around like a rapper's entourage. He was training them up to go out and do the work of bringing his kingdom. That is why the stories that follow in this book are so concerning. For a group of men whom Jesus chose to be the ones to change the world, they were a pretty dysfunctional, thick-headed bunch of dudes.

'You know who wouldn't have made so many mistakes? Women!' I hear you say. 'Why didn't Jesus pick any women? Was he sexist?'

I don't know if women would have done any better a job of being the Twelve than the men did. Maybe they would have made fewer mistakes, maybe they would have just made different ones, but it does seem like Jesus should have been an equal opportunity Messiah.

I think Jesus' choice of twelve men as disciples was a reflection of the twelve tribes of Israel. Each man was a correlation with the twelve fathers of those tribes; each of the Twelve was a new 'patriarch' for the new people of God.

Another reason why the Twelve were all male was probably because in Jewish society Jesus needed ten men to be accepted as a rabbi (a Jewish religious teacher). A Jewish synagogue couldn't meet without having ten men present. The Twelve were an authentication of his religious authority, even for those people who disagreed with him.[2]

---

2. If you would like to read more about this, you could check out Marg Mowczko's article on this topic: https://margmowczko.com/the-twelve-apostles-were-all-male/

That said, Jesus did have female disciples, they just weren't in the Twelve. Some of these women were Mary Magdalene, Mary the wife of Clopas, Mary the Mother of Jesus, Joanna, and Susanna. They travelled with Jesus and supported his ministry (Luke 8:1–3), served him and learned from him (Luke 10:38–42), were with Jesus at his crucifixion (Luke 23:49; John 19:25–27), and were the first people to proclaim the resurrection after being brave enough to visit Jesus' tomb (Luke 24:1–12). Unfortunately, for the purposes of this book, these women aren't recorded in the Bible doing a lot of stupid things, so they won't get many mentions in the following pages. That said, having met at least one or two women, I know that they can also make daft decisions. Stupidity is not gendered. So hopefully, if you're a woman, you'll be able to identify with the poor choices of the Twelve, while also being encouraged by your Jesus-following sisters who give womankind such a good name in the Gospels.

The Twelve

So, who were these twelve men specifically? These are the names that Mark gives us: 'These are the twelve he appointed: Simon (to whom he gave the name Peter), James son of Zebedee and his brother John (to them he gave the name Boanerges, which means "sons of thunder"), Andrew, Philip, Bartholomew, Matthew, Thomas, James son of Alphaeus, Thaddaeus, Simon the Zealot and Judas Iscariot, who betrayed him' (Mark 3:16–19).

There are a few other lists of the disciples throughout the New Testament. All of them have a similar structure, though some of the names are different. Before you get worried about some vast conspiracy of the Catholic Church to cover up some of the disciples, or that Christianity is all bunk because the writers of the Bible didn't even know who Jesus' disciples were, let me allay your fears: in all likelihood, there were a few disciples who had multiple names; the Gospels were written in Greek, the disciples spoke Aramaic, and the region they lived in had Hebrew, Greek, and Roman cultures (to name just the big ones); and Jesus gave at least a few of them new names. So, throw all that into the mix, and you're going to get a few people being called different things. As an example, as a young man I used to love the Hong Kong film star, Jackie Chan. His actual name is Chan Kong-sang, but when he was living in Australia working on construction sites, some of us Aussies struggled with the name Kong-sang. So people started calling him 'Little Jack', the name stuck, and he became Jackie.[3] This story highlights the casual racism of 1970s Australia, but it also illustrates my point: sometimes people can be known by different things because of various cultural idiosyncrasies, but that doesn't mean that they're two different people. If one list of Jesus' disciples listed a Kong-sang, and another listed Jackie, you'd now be comfortable that they're both the same person.

---

3. I learned this from Wikipedia, and couldn't track down a better source for the info, so take it with a grain of Wikipedia: https://en.wikipedia.org/wiki/Jackie_Chan#Early_life

Alright, now that we've got all that out of the way, let's get on with this list of the disciples:[4]

Simon Peter

Simon (who was given the name Peter by Jesus) was a fisherman by trade. I know this because that's what the Bible says, but also because my parents read my older sister and me a book about him when we were kids called *The Big Fisherman.* His family came from a town called Bethsaida (which means Fishertown, in case you were wondering) but he had a house in Capernaum. The family fishing business was on the Sea of Galilee. Simon Peter had a wife. Though she never gets a walk-on role in the Bible, we know she existed because he had a mother-in-law (Mark 1:29–31) and Paul mentions that Peter used to take his wife with him on ministry trips (1 Corinthians 9:5). As we'll see in the book, he was a guy who was often impulsive and said the first thing that popped into his mind. I'm sure you know people like him. You may even be a person like him yourself.

James

James was the older brother of John and son of Zebedee (which is a cool name if you ask me). Like Peter, he came from Bethsaida, and his family also had a fishing business on the Sea of Galilee in partnership with Simon Peter's family. There is also a chance that James and John were

---

4. For the following biographical info, I'm relying mainly on *Dictionary of Jesus and the Gospels, Second Edition,* ed. J. B. Green, J. K. Brown, & N. Perrin (Nottingham: IVP Academic, 2013).

Jesus' cousins. Jesus gave James and John the nickname 'sons of thunder', which was not a motorcycle gang, a comment on their parents, or a reference to what happened when they went to the bathroom. It was because they were rather impetuous. As we'll see in Chapter 8, they were partial to blowing stuff up. They also didn't mind making totally inappropriate requests of Jesus (see Chapter 11).

John

John was the younger brother of James and the son of Zebedee. Like James, he may also have been Jesus' cousin. If that is the case, then Jesus had at least two cousins with the name John, which would have made family Christmases very confusing.[5] John is also thought to be the writer of the book of John and the person referred to in that book as 'the disciple whom Jesus loved'. This could be because he thought he was the favourite but more likely because he knew deeply what it meant to be loved by Jesus.

Andrew

Andrew was Peter's brother. He too grew up in Bethsaida and was also a fisherman in the family business. Before Jesus turned up, Andrew was a disciple of John the Baptist. Throughout the Gospels, Andrew was often bringing people to meet Jesus (John 1:41–42; 6:8; 12:22). There isn't a lot of other information about Andrew, but let's assume that no news is good news.

5. I know they wouldn't have celebrated Christmas.

Philip

Philip was also from the town of Bethsaida. He and
the other four disciples from Bethsaida would have all
known each other (it was a small town), and there is
a chance they called themselves the Bethsaida Boys.[6]
The only Gospel where Philip gets a speaking role is the
book of John. Perhaps John liked letting his hometown
buddies play a role in his book.

Bartholomew

Young Barty was the son of Talmay (that's what
Bartholomew means). He may also have been known as
Nathanael, whom we meet in John's Gospel. The Bible
doesn't tell us that, but we can guess this might be the
case because Bartholomew is never mentioned in John's
Gospel, and Nathanael is never mentioned in Matthew,
Mark, or Luke. Nathanael, was said by Jesus to have 'no
deceit' in him, which is a pretty good endorsement to get
from the king of the universe (John 1:47).

Matthew

Matthew, also known as Levi, was a tax collector.
His occupation is just about all we know about him.
He was called by Jesus to follow him right out of his
tax-collecting booth (Mark 2:13–17). Given what we
know about how much tax collectors were disliked by
the general population because of their support of the

---

6. I have no evidence they actually called themselves that, but I
assume if they did all the other disciples would have found it very
annoying.

Roman oppressors, he may not have been too popular among the other disciples. Matthew is also thought to be the author of the book of Matthew.

Thomas

Thomas was also known as Didymus, which means twin. We have no idea who his twin was. Some people like to think that Thomas was Jesus' twin. There are all sorts of interesting theological questions about how a twin would work with a divine conception, but there is no evidence in the Bible that Jesus had a twin and that the twin was Thomas. (That said, Jesus did have plenty of brothers and sisters, including James who wrote the book of James.) Thomas did doubt Jesus' resurrection (you can be sure we're going to talk about that – see Chapter 14), but he was also the disciple who was prepared to die with Jesus when he had no idea what he was getting himself into (John 11:16), so we shouldn't give Thomas a bad rap.

James son of Alphaeus

James had a father named Alphaeus. That's about the extent of our knowledge of this bloke. We know he was the son of Alphaeus only to distinguish him from James the son of Zebedee. It also distinguishes him from James the brother of Jesus. There were a lot of Jameses floating around the ancient world.

Thaddaeus

Thaddaeus was probably also known as Judas, but not *that* Judas. He was Judas son of James, but not *those*

26

Jameses (I told you there was a lot of Jameses). It would be annoying if your main claim to fame was to be called 'the other Judas', but he was still one of Jesus' disciples, so that's not a bad thing to tell the kids. Better than being the fifth Wiggle, who left the original Wiggles just before they got rich and famous.

Simon the Zealot

Simon was a zealot, which doesn't mean he cared a lot about stuff. It could be he was called this because he was very devoted to his religion. However, there was a particular political movement called the Zealots (not to be confused with the band from Surrey, England, of the same name). The Zealots were a 'nationalist Jewish group that was willing to engage in active resistance against the Romans'.[7] They probably didn't exist until around AD 66, so Simon couldn't have been one when he was hanging out with Jesus, but the Gospel writers may have called him 'the Zealot' because the Zealots were around when they were writing the Gospels so their readers would have known what they were talking about. If that was the case, you can be sure that there would have been at least some tension between Simon the Israelite nationalist and Matthew, the guy who raised funds for Israel's Roman oppressors.

Judas Iscariot

Judas was from the town of Kariot. He also was also probably pretty good with money because he was made

---

7. E. J. Schnabel, 'Apostle', in *Dictionary of Jesus and the Gospels*, 42.

the treasurer of the disciples (John 13:29). I've devoted a whole chapter to Judas later in the book, so I won't say much more here, except to say this: the only thing worse than being known as 'not *that* Judas', would be to be known as 'yes, *that* Judas'.

On with the show

So there you have it, the twelve disciples who were chosen to be with Jesus, preaching and driving out demons. Now that we've met all the major characters (and some quite minor ones too, it seems), we can get on with this adventure. While these guys might do a lot of stupid stuff, I hope you'll be far from disappointed in what they have to teach us. As we look at their stories, we'll see what we can learn about ourselves and about Jesus. We'll see how God changed them and used them. If I do my job right, you'll have a laugh, you'll identify with the disciples, and, by the power of God, you'll become a little more like Jesus, so that you too might change the world.

Are you ready?

1

ORIGIN STORIES

The First Disciples
John 1:35-51

I had a privileged childhood. If you met me and saw my humble demeanour, you wouldn't know it, but my parents were very rich. In the city where I grew up, they were famous for their tremendous wealth and generosity to charity and those in need. As a kid, I spent much of my free time exploring the giant estate that we lived on and the caves beneath my house. I was a cheerful kid, only scared of the creatures that lived in the dark of those caves.

One day when I was not yet a teenager, my parents took me to the theatre. That night, as we were leaving via the back alley, a man held us up at gunpoint. I still remember the screams as my father tried to protect my mother, but in doing so, they were both shot and killed. I was shattered. I vowed to devote my life to fighting crime in my city so that no child would ever witness what I had witnessed. I now spend my nights dressed as a creature of the night, sitting on rooftops and protecting my city as best I can.

Okay. You figured it out. That's not my story. I stole it from the famous comic book hero, Man Who Dresses as a Bat. My origin story is much less interesting. My parents weren't particularly wealthy, and not once were they murdered. They still live in the house I grew up in in Sydney's Northern Suburbs. I could tell you about my childhood, but in the big scheme of things, it was mostly unremarkable. Chances are, your origin story isn't that exciting either (though if it is, that's fine; I just hope it doesn't resemble Bruce Wayne's too much). This book is about Jesus' disciples, who were unremarkable people. At least, they started out as unremarkable people. None of them were famous or powerful. They might have gone on to change the world, write much of the New Testament, and have churches all over the world named after them, but they weren't always the spiritual giants that we know them as. They started out as inauspicious young men. As inauspicious as you or me. These are their origin stories.

First meetings

Before we meet the disciples in the Gospel of John (which is the biography of Jesus traditionally thought to have been written by the disciple named John), we meet Jesus' cousin, John the Baptist (a different John from the disciple John who may have written the book of John – too many Johns!), who had been telling people that Jesus was on the way. John had his own entourage of disciples, and when along came Jesus, it prompted John to yell out to them, 'Look, the Lamb of God!' (John 1:36). Everyone looked around, trying to see the promised Messiah, or perhaps hoping for some magical lamb, and they saw Jesus, a carpenter from Nazareth. I don't know how you'd feel if that happened.[8] Imagine you've been following John, who has been talking for months about how the great man of God will come along soon, how he is going to change everything, and then along comes a plumber in high-vis. I've got nothing against tradespeople – I just usually expect tradespeople to build a fence, paint a house, or unblock a toilet rather than save the world.[9]

_____

8. If you're wondering, the word 'Messiah' means 'anointed one'. The people of Israel had ancient prophesies that one day a king would come along to rescue them from oppression and rule Israel for eternity. They spent a lot of time looking and hoping for when the Messiah would turn up. To proclaim that Jesus was the Messiah was a big deal.

9. We don't learn that Jesus is a carpenter in John, but in Mark 6:3. The word for carpenter in Greek didn't just mean someone who built houses or wooden furniture. It could have meant someone who was a builder, a stonemason, or some other type of craftsmen. They could be well-respected business people. So perhaps it would be better to imagine it more like meeting a bloke who owns a successful building company. The role of tradies in our society is different to the role they played in ancient Israel, so the first disciples may have had no qualms about following a carpenter. Still, I thought the idea of a plumber in high-vis saving the world was funny, so I've put the more factual info into this footnote.

Despite this, at least two of John's disciples were willing to accept that Jesus was the Messiah foretold in the ancient Scriptures. So, they ran after him. Jesus immediately turned around and, speaking his first words in the book, asked them, 'What do you want?' (v. 38).

John the Baptist's two disciples (one whom we learn was Andrew, and the other could have been John) seemed a little bit thrown off by this question. So they said, '"Rabbi" (which means "Teacher"), "where are you staying?"' (v. 38). I don't know why they asked that question. Were they really so interested in seeing Jesus' accommodation? When I was a kid and had to play at some other kids' place, the initial minutes were always pretty awkward, so the first question would often be, 'Can you show me your bedroom?' and then we'd go stand in their room still feeling just as weird, but now in their room. I'd inspect their Lego and action figures before we eventually remembered how to play with other humans. Perhaps these two disciples were hoping to see Jesus' Lego and action figures to break the tension.

Jesus indulged them and took them to see his place, where he probably showed them his favourite skateboard and talked about what it's like to be a new-on-the-scene Messiah.

Andrew had such a good time playing at Jesus' place that he rushed off to find his brother Simon to tell him about his new friend. Andrew did what became the most effective way for anyone to find out about Jesus: he told his friends and family about him. For millennia to come, followers of Jesus have found the people they know and love and said to them, 'I've found the Messiah!' hoping they might meet him too.

Simon went with his brother, and when Jesus saw him, Jesus knew him. He said, '"You are Simon son of John. You will be called Cephas" (which, when translated, is Peter)' (v. 42).

Now if this were a movie, for instance, the prequel to a film about the life of Peter the Apostle, there might be a collective gasp among the audience as we realise this is Peter, and this is how he got his name. But if you were actually Simon/Peter, you might not be so impressed. Imagine you met this guy, and straight away he gave you a new name. If I met someone and they said to me, 'You are Thomas son of Vernon. You will be called Grant', I would be pretty upset.[10] I quite like my name, and I don't really want some guy I've just met deciding to name me as someone else.

However, what Jesus was doing in giving Simon a new name was telling him who he will become. Names are pretty significant in the Bible. These days we put little stock in names; a name is just a name and it doesn't have a lot of bearing on your life. If Jesus wanted to give a new name to Simon today, he could take an online poll and then end up naming him Disciple McDiscipleface, everyone would have a laugh, and that would be that. But in the Bible, a name tells you who you are. Moses' name meant 'Draw out' because he was drawn out of the water, but also because he would draw God's people

10. My dad's name really is Vernon, but everyone calls him... you guessed it... John.

out of slavery (Exodus 2:10). Jacob's name means 'He deceives' (Genesis 25:26), and he spent much of his life deceiving people until God changed his name to Israel, which means 'He struggles with God' (Genesis 32:28). God's name is Yahweh, which means 'I am', the short version of 'I am who I am', which is God saying that he is so unique and beyond comprehension that he is defined only by himself (Exodus 3:14). Jesus' name means 'Yahweh Saves' because it is by him that God saves his people.

So Jesus decided Simon should be known by a different name. Simon was a pretty common name; it was the name of one of the twelve tribes of Israel, so there were people all over the place called Simon. But Jesus gave Simon a brand new name. His name was to be Peter. Peter means 'Rock' or 'Rocky'. Which is actually a pretty good name to receive, much better than if, for instance, Jesus called him 'Stove' or 'Compost'. Jesus saw who Simon would become; not just a fisherman leading a quiet life in the small fishing town of Bethsaida, but a rock, a foundation for God's work in the world.[11] We'll talk more about that in Chapter 6. Right from the beginning, Jesus knew the end of the story. No matter how bad things looked along the way (and they were going to look pretty bad at times), Jesus knew who Peter was going to become. God was going to do an important work in Simon, so that the man who finished the journey would not be the same man

---

11. F. F. Bruce, *The Gospel of John* (Grand Rapids: Eerdmans, 1983), 59.

who started it. He would no longer be just a common Simon but an uncommon Rock.

The following day, Jesus headed off to Galilee, and along the way he found Philip (whose name means 'Lover of Horses', just while we're talking about names) and he straight up said to him, 'Follow me'. Philip thought, 'Fair enough', and followed Jesus. This seems pretty quick. Maybe Phil had been studying the Scriptures and recognised a Messiah when he saw one, or maybe he just got a good vibe from Jesus.

Philip went off in search of his mate Nathanael and told him, 'We have found the one Moses wrote about in the Law, and about whom the prophets also wrote – Jesus of Nazareth, the son of Joseph' (John 1:45). He was telling Nathanael that they've met the one from all the ancient prophecies. But Nathanael was sceptical. He said, 'Nazareth! Can anything good come from there?' (v. 46). Nazareth didn't have a very good reputation; you wouldn't really expect a Messiah to come from there. Not because it was bad – it was just small. If the Messiah were to turn up today, you might expect them to be from somewhere important like New York, or London, or Beijing, but what if someone said, 'The Messiah from Holbrook is here!'? You'd probably say, 'Holbrook! Can anything good come from there?' Or you'd have no idea where Holbrook even is.[12] There

---

12. In which case, you should google it. But just in case you don't, it's in inland New South Wales about halfway between Sydney and Melbourne. It also has a submarine in a park, which is an excellent thing to see hundreds of kilometres away from the closest ocean.

isn't anything wrong with it – it's just not the sort of place you'd expect someone as significant as the Messiah to come from.

Philip wasn't having any of Nathanael's geographic elitism, so he convinced Nathanael to at least meet Jesus. When they got there, Jesus saw Nathanael and said, 'Here truly is an Israelite in whom there is no deceit' (v. 47).

Nathanael, perhaps feeling a little weirded out, said, 'How do you know me?' to which Jesus responded, 'I saw you while you were still under the fig-tree before Philip called you' (v. 48).

This was a strange thing to say. Jesus was proving that he really knew who Nathanael was. Now, I have no idea what Nathanael was doing under the fig tree. I used to think this meant that Nathanael was up to something dodgy under the fig tree. Like if today Jesus said, 'I saw you when you were on your phone alone in your room last night.' This feels like a 'Jesus even sees your incognito tab' moment – Nathanael should have used a VPN. But I think that's probably not what's going on. Immediately before he told Nathanael he had seen him, Jesus said Nathanael was 'an Israelite in whom there is no deceit' (v. 47). You don't say that about someone looking at ancient porn hiding behind a tree.[13]

So, I shouldn't be that down on the town. It's my favourite place to stop when I drive between Sydney and Melbourne.

13. I don't know a lot about ancient nudie magazines and decided against researching it because the government is watching, but going from memory I think the Greeks were pretty keen on drawing naked people on the side of clay pots, so perhaps it was more

So what was Nathanael doing? Assuming Jesus wasn't being ironic in his praise, it was probably something commendable. Maybe he had a particularly earnest prayer session pledging his life to God; maybe he discovered a bag of money and chose not steal it; maybe he found an ancient nudie mag and didn't sneak a peek. Whatever went on under the branches of that tree, Jesus saw and approved. Jesus saw Nathanael for who he was.

Jesus' insight convinced Nathanael: 'Rabbi, you are the Son of God; you are the king of Israel' (v. 49).

Jesus responded by saying, 'You believe because I told you I saw you under the fig-tree. You will see greater things than that... Very truly I tell you, you will see "heaven open, and the angels of God ascending and descending on" the Son of Man' (vv. 50–51).[14] Jesus was

---

likely that he would have found porno pottery. If you find that you are regularly tempted to look at porn pots, make sure you tell someone and set up some accountability structures. Too many young people these days are getting addicted to archaeologically uncovered ancient drawings of the ancients uncovered.

14. You may be wondering what 'Son of Man' means, and why it is used in reference to Jesus, especially when he is the only person, apart from Adam and the clones of the future, who specifically did not have a man as their biological father. At the risk of over simplification of an important concept, the phrase 'Son of Man' is a reference to Daniel 7 where there is a prophesy about 'one like a son of man, coming with the clouds of heaven'. This Son of Man is human, hence being a son of man, but also is worshipped and has divine authority (vv. 13–14).

When Jesus refers to himself as the 'Son of Man' he is taking this title for himself and claiming his role as the one prophesied about in Daniel 7. He is both human and God, with divine authority and who is worthy of worship. So Jesus is not just talking about

making a reference to the story in Genesis 28 where Jacob had a dream and saw angels going up and down a stairway from heaven to earth. After the dream Jacob woke up and said: 'Surely the Lord is in this place, and I was not aware of it. How awesome is this place! This is none other than the house of God; this is the gate of heaven' (vv. 16,17). He then named the place Bethel, which means 'House of God'. Jacob was very impressed that he had encountered God on earth.

Jesus seems to be saying to Nathanael that he is the place where people can meet God. Knowing what Nathanael did in secret might be impressive, but in Jesus they will see God himself. Jesus is the 'house of God'; that is, he is where humanity meets God. A God-man? That is even more impressive than a bit of fig tree prophecy.

And with that, Jesus met five of his twelve disciples: Andrew, another guy who was probably John, Simon Peter, Philip, and Nathanael. While they probably didn't officially start following Jesus till later, Jesus was revealing himself to them and drawing them to himself. This was the start of their lifelong journey with Jesus.

What I love about this story is the way it encapsulates so much of what happens when any of us follow Jesus. Some people come to know Jesus because something amazing happens – a miracle, a vision, or a dream. But most of us come to know Jesus the same way these disciples did, because someone who knows and loves

his parentage but making a bold claim about his true identity, authority, and power.

us told us about him. In my case, it was my parents. They brought me up hearing about Jesus. They taught me about Jesus as they taught me about everything else in the world: 'The stove is hot, the sun is bright, Jesus is Lord.' Other people have sisters and brothers who tell them about Jesus, or friends who invite them to youth group or camp. Some people have people who they barely know share Jesus with them, just because they think Jesus is worth knowing. Then there are those poor people who get invited to a 'party' hoping for free drinks, only to discover it's a Christian event with only water and weak cordial on offer, and they've been tricked into listening to a talk about Jesus by some guy in Crocs, and, miraculously, they still find Jesus compelling.

Now, you might not yet have met Jesus. Maybe I'll get to be one of those people who introduces you to Jesus – that's exciting! You may have been given this book by someone who loves you and wants you to meet Jesus. Why? Because they've met Jesus and know he's worth knowing. Like Andrew and Philip, they've found Jesus compelling, and they hope you will discover what they've discovered. I hope you will too.

You want to know one of the reasons why Jesus is compelling? Because, like we saw in that first chapter of John's Gospel, when you meet Jesus, like with Nathanael, he knows who you are and, like with Simon Peter, he knows who you're going to be. Knowing exactly who you are, he still wants you to know him.

Jesus knows where you've been

When Jesus met Nathanael, Jesus knew him. He knew his heart and he knew what Nathanael had been up to in secret.

I don't know about you, but for me being 'known' isn't always something that I really like the idea of. I get a bit concerned about people seeing what I've been listening to on Spotify, so the idea of Jesus publicly naming my secrets is pretty scary. Sometimes I find myself in Christian meetings where, after a time of singing, there is a time of 'waiting on the Spirit', and then someone will stand up with a 'word' from God to share with everyone. I'll be sitting there thinking, 'Don't be for me, don't be for me.' I worry God will have shared with them one of my many sins, and they're going to stand up and tell everyone the worst things I've ever done.

But that isn't the way Jesus works. He's not into public shaming. He's not even into private shaming. Notice with Nathanael he doesn't say, 'Here's a guy who pretends to be humble but actually thinks he's better than everyone else.' Or 'I saw you steal your uncle Benjamin's money when no one was around.' Though I'm sure he could easily have revealed all of Nathanael's secret sins. Instead, he highlighted Nathanael's integrity and shared a secret moment that reflected well on Nathanael. Despite his ability to do otherwise, Jesus was gentle with Nathanael and built him up.

And Jesus knows you, too. He knows what you got up to under your fig tree. He knows your secret devotion, and he knows your hidden sins. He knows your anxieties, and he knows your desires. He knows the things you have done, and he knows what others have done to you. He knows you. He knows you better than you know yourself. Now this might be a fearful prospect for you, but Jesus doesn't know you and despise you, and he isn't interested in condemning you for your sin (John 8:1–11; Romans 8:1). Jesus knows you, and he loves you. Jesus knows you, and he calls you to follow him. In the book of Ephesians, we're told that God chose his people before the creation of the world (Ephesians 1:4). That means that, before the universe even existed, we who put our trust in Jesus, were known, loved, and chosen.[15]

Sometimes we make friends with people and then realise, after getting to know them, we don't actually like them very much. We then try to figure out how to avoid them. Sometimes people do the same to us.

This is the wonderful thing about Jesus knowing us when he meets us: he isn't going to get to know us and then regret having us as his follower. There is no cooling off period with Jesus. He knows us, he loves us, he likes us, and he wants to be our friend.

Jesus knows where you're going

Jesus doesn't just know who you are; he knows who you're going to become. Jesus knew ordinary Simon

---

15. 'But... um... Tom, you're talking about predestination. This is stressing me out.' I don't really want to get into predestination here because we'll get sidetracked, but feel free to jump on the YouTubes and search 'twfrench predestination' if you want to know what I think.

would become Peter, the rock. He knew he was going to be transformed. I don't want to give you any spoilers, but all the disciples were transformed. And the promise of the Bible is that all who put their trust in Jesus are changed. The Holy Spirit works in us, changing our character so that we might become more like Jesus. Paul (who himself was dramatically transformed) talks about this hope in his letter to the Philippians when he says he is confident 'that he who began a good work in you will carry it on to completion until the day of Christ Jesus' (Philippians 1:6).

Who you are now is not who you will always be. When Jesus chooses you to follow him, he does it knowing who you are and who you'll become. Peter's transformation from Simon to Peter was not a straight climb from lowly fisherman to superhero apostle. As we're going to see, he had many difficulties along the way, but Jesus remained committed to him the whole time.

You might look at yourself at any moment in time and despair that you are not the person you want to be. But who you are is not who you will become. Jesus hasn't finished his work in you. He knows who you are, and he knows who you are becoming, and he's committed to you the whole time. Jesus doesn't call the wrong people. As long as Jesus is with you, you've got an exciting journey ahead of you. He knows you, and he's not done with you, not by a long shot. Hold on tight; it's going to be a wild ride.

2

NAPPING AND SCREAMING

Jesus Calms the Storm
Mark 4:35–41

Once, a chicken almost killed me. It's quite rare that I find myself in a life-threatening situation, but this one time, with this one chicken, it happened to me.

I was eating dinner with my friend, Howie. I'd cooked us up an amazing feast of sweet and sour chicken. I had used my brilliant chef skills to follow all the instructions on the jar of sweet and sour sauce. We chatted as we ate, and Howie said something particularly funny. Usually, his jokes are not a problem. I just laugh and try to think of my own funny joke to prove that I'm as funny as him. But this time, when he told the joke, I had just put a piece of chicken in my mouth, and that was a problem.

Here's some science for you: when you laugh you need to get air, and to get air you suck it into your lungs through your mouth or your nose. When I needed to laugh, all my bodily functions performed as they should: I breathed in air in preparation to let out my raucous laughter, but as I breathed in air, I also breathed in chicken. One significantly large piece of chicken got lodged in my windpipe, which (in case you never paid attention in science) is the wrong pipe for chicken. No one has ever successfully digested sweet and sour chicken in their lungs.

Suddenly, the airflow to my lungs plummeted by 98.6 per cent. Lights and warning sirens sounded in my brain's control room.[16] I ran through the various ways to save myself from the killer chicken. I had recently done first aid training, so I knew that the best thing to do with a choking person was to throw them over a chair and whack them on the back. I thought this through and realised I couldn't do this to myself, and I also had no way to tell Howie to do it for me, because I had no air, thus no ability to speak.

I raced to the kitchen sink, shoved my fingers down my throat, and tried to make myself vomit. I wasn't sure if this was the right thing to do, but I was pretty sure dying was the wrong thing to do. As I retched over the sink, it occurred to me that I might die. Right there in the kitchen, I could die of chicken. That was not how I wanted to go. I haven't yet decided what my ideal death

16. Pretty sure that's a thing because I saw it in that movie, *Inside Out*.

is, though I am relatively sure it doesn't involve sweet and sour chicken and one of Howie's jokes.

Happily, I didn't die. My vomit induction skills worked, and I spewed the killer chicken chunk into the sink. I sat back down at the table, limbs shaking, adrenaline pumping, happy to still be alive. I would live on to laugh at another joke.[17]

Now that I have had my near-death experience, when I read the story of Jesus calming the storm, I like to think I know something of the feelings of the disciples. Perhaps choking on chicken brings out a similar type of fear to being stuck in a boat in the middle of a deadly storm. However, what the disciples had, which I did not, was Jesus, physically, right there with them in the storm.

The disciples go sailing with Jesus

This story begins when Jesus and his disciples get in a boat. Jesus had been doing some teaching about what the kingdom of God is like, and at the end of the day they all hopped in a boat to head off across the lake of Galilee – the same lake that Jesus met the disciples beside when he first called them to follow him. This lake features pretty regularly in the early stories of Jesus.

So, they headed out on the boat and Mark 4:37 says, 'A furious squall came up'. Squall sounds to me

---

17. I realise I began the story by saying 'a chicken almost killed me' when as you now know, in truth, a *piece* of chicken almost killed me. The chicken was already dead so it had no will of its own to try to kill me. But 'a chicken almost killed me' sounds a lot more dramatic than 'a piece of chicken almost killed me'. I'm not above a bit of exaggeration to make you keep reading my book.

like some sort of seagull. I get images of Jesus battling a giant, angry seagull, which would be awesome, but alas, that is not what squall means. A furious squall is a large storm.

This squall caused so many waves to break over the boat that it was nearly swamped (v. 37). The disciples freaked out, sure they were going to die. This is significant because, if you remember, many of these guys were fishermen; they'd grown up on the lake. They would have been taught to fish there by their fathers, who were taught to fish on that lake by their fathers before them. If sailing on the lake is in your blood, you know when to be afraid.

Meanwhile, in the back of the boat, Jesus slept (v. 38). Jesus had some next level napping skills. I like a nap as much as anyone. There is nothing more satisfying than a Sunday afternoon sleep. But if I even hear my phone vibrate, I'm awake. The nap is done. My wife, however, is a much more skilled napper. I can be watching TV or crashing about in the kitchen, and her nap continues, unabated. The other day she napped through our fire alarm as it blared at us and a stern man over the loudspeaker commanded, 'This is an emergency. Evacuate now!' One day, I might try to take her out on a boat while she's napping. But I doubt that even she would be able to sleep through the storm that Jesus slept through. That was a particularly powerful nautical nap.

Why was Jesus able to do this? I suspect a day of preaching to thousands of people wears a guy out (I get tired just trying to dictate a text message to my phone).

46

But to sleep through a storm that had seasoned fishermen crying out in fear? That required something else. Jesus' ability to sleep through the storm probably stemmed not just from tiredness but also from his trust in his Father. He knew that God the Father would never let him face anything which was beyond his care and control. The storm may have looked scary, but he was in a boat, on his Father's lake, in his Father's storm. He could sleep easy.

My little sister has an intellectual disability. Among other things, it means that she perceives the world differently. One time, she was on a flight from Sydney to Melbourne that encountered severe turbulence. I wasn't there, but I have been told that a lot of the passengers were pretty scared, crying out in fear whenever they experienced a big bump or drop. My sister, on the other hand, loved it! She thought it was an excellent ride. She laughed loudly as the plane bounced its way along. As it turns out, her enjoyment of the flight helped calm the other passengers down. It's harder to be afraid when the young woman with Down syndrome across the aisle from you is laughing with joy at the sheer fun of a bouncy flight. As well as thinking it was loads of fun, she had complete trust in the people caring for her, which meant that she wasn't afraid in the slightest. And she was completely right not to be afraid, because while she does not understand air crash statistics, and despite how others felt about their situation, they were in much less danger on the bumpy plane than in the car on the way to the airport to catch their flight. What the situation looked like and the reality of the situation were two different things. They didn't need to be afraid.

In the storm on the lake, the disciples could have taken a page out of Jesus' book. Like the passengers on the plane who took comfort in my sister's joy, they could have looked at Jesus, calmly asleep, and realised, 'If Jesus isn't worried, we don't need to worry.' But instead, they thought they knew better than Jesus, and woke him up. I'm unsure what outcome they were looking for. I doubt they hoped he'd calm the storm – Jesus hadn't given any indication that he possessed that kind of power yet. Perhaps they were only hoping that he'd panic with them. They woke him up and said, 'Teacher, don't you care if we drown?' (v. 38).

They came to the right guy, because instead of getting grumpy that he was woken by some panicked fishermen (and at least one tax collector), he got up and rebuked the wind and the waves, telling them, 'Quiet! Be still!' (v. 39).

And everything became calm.

Can you imagine being one of Jesus' disciples at that moment? They knew Jesus was impressive, but there he was speaking to the storm, and it became still! In my job I spend a lot of time speaking to groups of teenagers, and when I try to calm them down it can sometimes be very difficult – and teenagers have ears and the ability to stop talking and pay attention if they want to. I don't know if you're aware of this, but storms have no ability to listen to anyone, nor to make decisions about whether they storm or not. Storms just squall around oblivious of the fact that they even exist, let alone being able to hear a dude yelling at them to calm down. The weather is uncontrollable, yet here was a man who could control it.

Jesus then turned to his disciples and said, 'Why are you so afraid? Do you still have no faith?' (v. 40).

What kind of question was that? I reckon if I were a disciple, if I wasn't completely stunned by what had just happened, I would have wanted to shout at Jesus, 'Because we were going to die!' Being afraid in a situation like that seems entirely rational. In a fight between a carpenter turned travelling preacher-healer and a storm, my money is going to be on the storm every time.

Jesus' questions to the disciples weren't saying, 'Why were you so afraid? Of course, I was going to calm the storm.' Jesus makes no storm-quelling promises. Instead, he tells them they didn't need to panic because of his identity. That's why he asked, 'Do you still have no faith?' By this stage, he expected them to have learnt something more about who he was. They weren't hanging out with just anyone; they were following the Son of Man! John the Baptist's teaching about Jesus, when the disciples first met Jesus, made Jesus' identity clear, but the disciples hadn't figured it out. Jesus, in his healing miracles (which we haven't talked about, but you can find some of them in the first four chapters of Mark before this story – see Mark 2:1–12 in particular), made clear who he was. But the disciples hadn't understood.

49

But even if they hadn't yet figured out that Jesus was more than just some bloke who told good stories and who could heal, they at least might have taken a cue from Jesus as he slept. If Jesus is asleep while you're panicking, then one of you has the wrong response to the situation. If Jesus could trust his Father, then the disciples could too!

Despite all this, the disciples didn't understand. Rather than being comforted by the presence of Jesus, they were scared: 'They were terrified and asked each other, "Who is this? Even the wind and the waves obey him!"' (v. 41).

Once again, this seems like a perfectly reasonable response. If you had a friend from school and you found out they had built a nuclear missile in their back shed, you might be terrified. Even if you thought your friend was perfectly lovely, being around someone with that kind of power can make you wee your pants a little. So the disciples discovering their mate had the power to control the weather would make them concerned in case he ever turned that power on them.

They had seen his power, but they hadn't understood his heart. Until they truly understood his love for them, they wouldn't understand that they didn't need to be afraid.

Don't you care?

My guess is that you may see a little of yourself in the question the disciples asked: 'Teacher, don't you care if we drown?'

How often do we ask Jesus the question, 'Don't you care?' There can be times when we're facing all sorts of difficulties, and Jesus seems asleep, like he has no interest in our situation. For you, it could be when your parents are fighting, or someone you love is sick. Or perhaps you're wrestling with mental illness, or you're being bullied at school. When God doesn't intervene to fix your problems, you can feel like you've been abandoned and like Jesus is asleep.

But what was Jesus' response to the disciples? He calmed the storm then asked them, 'Why are you so afraid? Do you still have no faith?' He didn't promise that he would save them from every storm; they weren't meant to be unafraid because Jesus would always save them. Instead, they didn't need to be afraid because they were with Jesus. With Jesus, they were under his care. If Jesus sleeping in the back of the boat wasn't a sign that remaining calm was a totally valid option, then I don't know what is. Just as Jesus was able to trust his Father's care, they too could trust Jesus. When they were with Jesus, they didn't need to be afraid.

Jesus never promises to save us from the storms we face, but if he's with us it can totally change how we experience them.

Parties and storms

I don't like going to parties. I'm just too awkward. I'm terrible at making conversation and I never know how to start new ones. I'll be talking to someone and the conversation will die, and while I'm frantically trying to think of something to say to resuscitate our discussion, my conversational partner will say they're going to get a drink, then never come back. Suddenly I'm all alone. When this happens, I look around at the party and will rarely find any new people to talk to – every group of people looks too difficult to just slide on into. So, I pull out my phone and pretend to send someone a message. If people see me by myself, at least they'll see me sending a message and know that even if I'm a loner at the party, I have someone, somewhere, who I can message.

I spent most of my life till my early thirties as a single man. But when I got a girlfriend, many things changed. One thing that changed dramatically was parties. Soon after we started dating, my girlfriend, Emily (who is now my wife), asked me to go to her friend's mum's fiftieth. That sounded terrible. I didn't know her friend, and I didn't know her friend's mum, and I definitely didn't want to go to some stranger's fiftieth. But still I said I'd go, because new love compelled me, and I wanted to do the right thing.

When we were at the party, I realised everything was different because it wasn't the terrible, frightening experience I was used to. When the conversation died, Emily would think of something to say. When someone disappeared to get a drink, Emily would be right there with me. If everyone left, Emily was still there. The party became so much better because I had Emily by my side. She didn't save me from the party (in fact, she took me to the party), but she transformed how I experienced the party because she was there with me.

This is what it's like with Jesus. When we are going through life's storms, we still have to go through them. But having Jesus with us can transform how we experience them. Knowing you're not alone and that Jesus isn't going to let anything happen to you that is beyond his control, can change everything. It can give you the courage to go on, knowing Jesus is by your side. It can give you the strength to love, knowing Jesus won't abandon you. If Jesus is with you, you don't need to be afraid.

The greatest storm

All this may be true, but when we face the storms of life, we still find ourselves asking Jesus the same question as the disciples: 'Don't you care?' If Jesus cared, wouldn't he save us from storms? At least the biggest, most painful storms?

Jesus once faced a storm greater than any his disciples had ever faced. As he prepared himself to go to the cross and die, he spent time in prayer. When Jesus prayed, he knew his death was at hand and that he would experience unimaginable physical and spiritual pain. Yet he didn't shrink away. He prayed, '*Abba*, Father... everything is possible for you. Take this cup from me. Yet not what I will, but what you will' (Mark 14:36). Jesus, in the midst of his storm, entrusted himself to his Father, trusting his Father's will over his own. Then Jesus went to the cross, allowing himself to be killed, dying on your behalf and mine. He experienced the death that we deserve, so we might find forgiveness and life. His death as the Son of

53

God secured for us the right to become daughters and sons of God.

So does he care? Yes! Yes! Yes!

But caring for us and saving us from things that are painful are not the same thing. The promise of Jesus is not that he will save us from everything bad, but that he will always be with us (Matthew 28:20). It's the presence of Jesus, and the knowledge that he loves us, that transforms how we can experience the storms we face in our lives.

The disciples needed to know that they were not alone. They could trust Jesus, as he trusted his Father. As you confront your storms, know that you are not alone. Know that Jesus has not and will not abandon you. If Jesus is with you, you can face any storm.

3

HUNGRY PEOPLE ARE THE WORST

Jesus Feeds the Five Thousand
Mark 6:30–44

I was about ten years old when my church held a combined camp with a church down the road. During the camp they had a 'secret angel' program where each person received the name of someone else on camp for whom they had to secretly do kind things. We were encouraged to take their plates to the kitchen after a meal when they weren't looking, or write encouraging notes and hide them where they'd find them, or send someone else to go give them a massage on our behalf, which, in retrospect, seems a little creepy. The person I was to be an 'angel' for was a leader from the other church. It took me a while to figure out who he was, but when I did, I started racking my brains for something that I might do for him that would be secret angel worthy. But try as I might, I couldn't come up with anything. That is, until the last night.

On the last night, we had a messy games night. We played games that involved us shoving our faces into bowls of flour to find chocolate, or playing catch with eggs, or trying to find marbles in buckets full of cold spaghetti with our feet. If you've ever been to youth group, there is a good chance you've experienced one of these events. On that night, my team won, and we all received a prize. This was a particularly big deal because I have the hand-eye coordination of a shovel, so I never win prizes for anything involving any kind of physical activity. You can imagine my excitement at winning a prize then. To top it off, the prize was a Mars Bar. This was a luxury that I rarely got to enjoy.

That's when it struck me: this was my chance to do something as the secret angel. I could give the guy my Mars Bar. It was a splendid idea, but... I really loved Mars Bars. I couldn't have my Mars Bar and eat it too. Or could I? What if I only ate some of the Mars Bar? Then I would be able to give him the other half. I'd enjoy the delight of that caramelly, chocolatey goodness, and so would he! That is what I resolved to do. I ate half the Mars Bar, then snuck into the guy's room and left the other half on his pillow. I am sure that when he walked in and laid eyes on that half-eaten Mars Bar, he said to himself, 'Oh wow! I've been visited by an angel!' And as he enjoyed fifty per cent of my hard-won Mars Bar, he rested in the knowledge that someone was looking out for him.

I suspect this story says quite a lot about the character of ten-year-old me, which probably still exists in much-older me. I am a stingy guy. These days, I don't give people half-eaten chocolate bars, but I suspect when people talk about me behind my back they don't say, 'My goodness, Tom is such a generous guy.' I'm generous in the good Christian way of offering the last hot chip to everyone, but only because I want them to refuse out of politeness so I can take it for myself. If I invite people over for dinner, they'll get fed, but there isn't any kind of abundant feast, like what happens when my wife cooks. I'm as stingy as politeness allows. In my heart, I'm still the kid who wants to eat the entire Mars Bar himself. In my actions, I'm still giving away half the Mars Bar because I feel the social pressure to do so. Then I read this story of the disciples and I feel a little better. Because my stinginess seems to be a very similar kind of stinginess to that of the disciples. They're very reasonable, they don't do anything really inane, but they do try to set some boundaries. Jesus, however, is the unreasonable one. He displays exactly the character trait that is going to get him killed one day.

The hungry crowd

The story begins after the disciples have been sent out in pairs by Jesus on a training mission. As they went out, they 'preached that people should repent. They drove out many demons and anointed with oil many people who were ill and healed them' (Mark 6:12–13). When they got back, they had some impressive stories and all gathered around Jesus to tell their tales of demon battles and miraculous healings. But the disciples' mission trips had done nothing to dull the public's excitement about Jesus. So many people kept 'coming and going' (v. 31), presumably to get healed or get a blessing from Jesus, that the disciples didn't even have time to eat. Because of this, Jesus decided they should find a quiet place to rest. Retreat time with Jesus – finally the disciples would be able to eat, have a rest, and tell Jesus all about their ministry tour. They left by boat across the sea of Galilee to a deserted place.

Unfortunately, the crowds got wind of them leaving and ran around the lake to get there before them. The deserted place wasn't so deserted anymore. Mark doesn't tell us what was in the hearts of the disciples, but I can imagine when the boat pulled up and they saw all those people there, their hearts sank. The disciples were meant to be having a relaxing retreat alone with Jesus, but instead there were crowds of people who just wanted more from them. Couldn't they just rest?

What did Jesus do? Did he send them away? Did he say, 'Sorry folks, we're not doing any healings today, we're having a day off'? I'm sure that's what the disciples were hoping for, and it would be an entirely reasonable thing to do, but Jesus saw the people were 'like sheep without a shepherd' (v. 34), and he had compassion on the crowd and began to teach them. Imagine how frustrated the disciples may have been with Jesus. This was meant to be their downtime, and yet Jesus decided to do more ministry. Why wouldn't Jesus think of his disciples? This was the first indication of Jesus' unreasonable generosity. He was giving himself to the crowds from the depths of his compassion, when any reasonable person would just turn the crowds away in favour of getting some rest. But not Jesus. That's not how Jesus rolls.

As evening approached, the disciples went up to Jesus and said to him, 'This is a remote place... and it's already very late. Send the people away so that they can go to the surrounding countryside and villages and buy themselves something to eat' (vv. 35–36). I don't know exactly what the disciples were thinking. Perhaps they were concerned for the welfare of the crowds, or perhaps they had come up with an ingenious plan to get rid of them. If Jesus would not get rid of them on his own, they could use reason and logic to convince him to do it. They could point out to Jesus the obvious problem that there was no food, forcing him to send them home, and then the disciples could get their well-deserved rest.

However, if this was a ploy to get rid of the crowds, Jesus saw through it easily, and said to the disciples, 'You give them something to eat' (v. 37).

'Oh... hold on... what?' The disciples were aghast! How the heck were they meant to feed all those people? We are told at the end of the story there were five thousand men present – not to mention their wives, and their kids, and their kids' friends who they brought along with them. The disciples, understandably shocked, informed Jesus that his plan was completely out of the question: 'That would take more than half a year's wages! Are we to go and spend that much on bread and give it to them to eat?' (v. 37). Their plan had well and truly backfired.

This book may be about many of the stupid things the disciples did, but see how sensible the disciples are here? In this case, their reaction seems totally rational. They came to Jesus with a very reasonable problem (loads of people need food), and he proposed a very unreasonable solution (you feed them). It seemed as if Jesus thought they were walking around with the equivalent of almost $40,000 in their man bags.[18] Plus, where would they find the infrastructure to feed that many people? I have turned up to Maccas with fifty teenagers, and it has totally freaked the staff out. Imagine turning up with 100 times that many people – the Maccas employees would just quit.[19] Now imagine you're in the middle of nowhere with no money, no food, no shops, and no way of making food and Jesus just casually tells you to feed 20,000 people. Talk about unreasonable expectations.

Unfortunately for the disciples, they had just been on mission for Jesus where they had been sent out with 'nothing for the journey except a staff – no bread, no bag,

---

18. This is based on the median Australian full-time wage in 2018 of $1,463 per week, which works out to $38,038 for 26 weeks. https://www.abs.gov.au/ausstats/abs@.nsf/0/27641437D6 780D1FCA2568A9001393DF

19. For my non-Australian readers, 'Maccas' is Aussie for McDonald's.

no money in [their] belts' (Mark 6:8). While on mission for Jesus, they had seen God provide and work miracles through them. In telling the disciples to feed the crowd, Jesus was asking the disciples to continue in the same power they had when they were on mission for him. Feeding thousands of people when you're on mission for Jesus is not out of the question, but alas the disciples had not absorbed the lessons of God's miraculous power they should have learnt while on mission for the kingdom, so Jesus would have to do the miracle himself.

Jesus sent the disciples away to find out how much food was available, and among them they rustled together five loaves and two fish. Not a feast by anyone's standards. But Jesus had everyone sit down in groups of hundreds and fifties (which, incidentally, is the same way I organise the cash in my wallet), reminiscent of the way Moses organised Israel into groups when he was its leader (Exodus 18:24–26). He then took the food. How would you have felt if you knew that was all the food you had? I can imagine the disciples looked longingly at the food as Jesus took it off them. But Jesus gave thanks to his Father in heaven and gave the food back to the disciples to distribute. As they did this, the miracle happened. Five loaves and two fish became ten loaves and four fish, which became twenty loaves and eight fish, which became forty loaves and sixteen fish, and on, and on, and on, until everyone had eaten and was satisfied. When the disciples picked up the leftovers there were twelve basketfuls left over, which, I don't need to tell you, was a lot more food than they started with.

A stingy God?

That is an amazing story! But do you see what I mean when I say the disciples behaved completely rationally? No one would expect that a small, personal picnic would feed the population of a reasonably sized country town. When Jesus asked the disciples to feed the crowd, it was an entirely unreasonable task for them to achieve on their own. Jesus might have just as easily invited them to go to the moon. But Jesus knew his request of the disciples was unreasonable. He's not stupid. He didn't seriously think they would be able to feed all those people on their own. He could have taken the disciples up on their suggestion to send the crowd away, but Jesus had the miraculous feeding in mind all along. He created the crisis, so he could create the solution too. Jesus didn't make the crowd hungry, but he used the fact of their hunger as an opportunity to show the disciples a little more of who he was.

Chances are, outside of the disciples, none of the people who ate that day were aware that they were eating miraculous bread. I assume it didn't glow or contain Pop Rocks (which probably would have counted as miraculous in ancient Israel). Jesus wanted to show the disciples something important about himself. If you've heard many Bible stories before, you may know that there are other miraculous feedings recorded in the Bible. When God's people were wandering around in the wilderness on their way to the Promised Land, God provided food from heaven so they wouldn't starve out in those deserted places (Exodus 16). And the prophet

Elisha once did a miracle very similar to Jesus', except he only fed 100 people with twenty loaves of bread (2 Kings 4:42–44). Jesus was teaching the disciples something about himself: just as God miraculously fed people through the prophets, here was Jesus feeding people in the wilderness. He was letting the disciples in on his true identity.

Greater than Moses, greater than the prophets, Jesus is the God who provides. And he provides abundantly! He is a generous God, who gives more than enough. He gives, and there is more left over to give.

How does this change your view of God? I'm not sure what you think of God, but I know I rarely think of him as being generous. I can easily feel like God is stingy.

When I'm not writing books, choking on chicken, or being stingy with Mars Bars, I spend a lot of time on YouTube. I don't watch the cool YouTubers; I watch a lot of nerdy plane videos. The ones I like the most are YouTubers' reviews of first class flights. I live vicariously through these men (they're almost always men) as they get to sleep on luxurious beds in the sky, have flight attendants at their beck and call, eat the nicest food, and drink the fanciest drinks. It looks like an amazing, extravagant adventure that I doubt I'll ever experience.

When I fly, I need to fly what I can afford, and at times that means flying with the super-cheap airlines who are the exact opposite of what I see on those videos. When you book, they try to squeeze every extra dollar out of you they can. Your seat might be $50, but if you want bags, or a window seat, or to sit with your friend, or to be guaranteed a spot on a plane and not on their 'premium plane replacement bus service' you are required to pay extra.[20] Then once it's time to fly, because they want to save as much money as possible, check-in at the airport is terrible. Instead of an easy check-in with friendly flight attendants, you're jammed into a check-in hall with hundreds of other grumpy people being yelled at by airline staff. The whole process takes so long that you find yourself running to your gate to catch your plane, only to discover that the plane is late. So you're stuck squeezed into the gate with the same grumpy people you just checked in with. Before you get on the plane, they weigh your hand luggage so they can charge you more than the price of your plane ticket if you want an extra kilo of stuff on the plane (and they know they're going to get money there, because nobody wanted to pay the extra money for baggage when they booked their ticket in the first place). Then you get on the plane and your seats are missing all reasonable legroom. The airline doesn't give you any food, but you can buy a depressed sandwich and miniature juice for $16. Don't even think of asking the flight attendant for anything unless you're willing to pay for it. By the time you get off the plane, you vow never to fly with them again. Until, of course, you get lured in by that cheap fare, and it all starts again.

Sometimes God seems to me like the low-cost airline. Never wanting to give you any more than he can get away with. And if you want something good from

20. Okay, I've never seen the replacement bus thing, but I wouldn't put it past them.

God, it will cost you. It'll cost you in prayer, obedience, happiness, or comfort. Or maybe, even if you pray and do the right thing, God isn't going to give you what you want anyway.

But that isn't the picture of God we witness in this story. Here, Jesus shows us the character of God as a giver. When Jesus saw the crowds, he didn't turn them away. He was generous with his emotions, feeling compassion for them. He was generous with his time as he taught the crowds. And then he went over and above in his generosity as he gave more than enough to feed the thousands who were in need before him.

Jesus was showing God's true heart. And this wasn't a one-off event, this is what we observe of God again, and again, and again. Ultimately, we see it when Jesus gave his life at the cross so we might receive eternal life. That is radical generosity, Jesus gave all of himself for us.

What this means is that whatever views we hold, a stingy God doesn't stack up against the evidence. A God who died for us is not a God who will refuse us anything we need. As Romans 8:32 says: 'He who did not spare his own Son, but gave him up for us all – how will he not also, along with him, graciously give us all things?'

'But what about the fact that I prayed and prayed but God didn't answer?' you may be asking. If God is generous, why doesn't he give us what we want? I'm guessing if you've ever heard any teaching on this you know the generic answer: 'If a kid asks for lollies every day, a good parent isn't going to give it to them.' The reason you've probably heard it before is because it's true. Love means sometimes not giving the person what they want. I'm very thankful that God hasn't given me everything that I have asked for. I haven't married every person who I have prayed to marry. I haven't got the successful but hollow careers that I've asked for. I haven't made the millions of dollars that I've hinted to God he should give me. If God answered all my selfish prayers, he wouldn't be a loving, fatherly God, but my slave. I need God, not a slave.

You could come back at me with, 'Yes, but not every prayer is selfish. What about healing or people coming to faith in Jesus? Why won't a generous God answer those?' To be honest with you, I'm not sure why God doesn't answer the seemingly good prayers. There are some requests that seem like bread and fish to a starving person, and still God seems not to answer them. And while I could hazard a guess, I do not know the mind of God, I do not get to sit in on God's deliberations, so I should not attempt to explain what I do not understand.[21] But what can we be sure about? We know God is generous. Jesus wouldn't die for rebels like us if he was not entirely committed to us. So the way God answers your prayers cannot come from a place of indifference or malice. His answer, however perplexing, has come from the man who had compassion on the crowds, but who

---

21. If you would like a good resource for thinking about unanswered prayer, you may like to check out *God on Mute* by Pete Grieg. It's not always a happy read, but it's full of hard-won insights into God's character even when he seems unmoved by our needs or deepest desires. Pete Grieg, *God on Mute* (Brighton: David C Cook, 2020).

also used the hunger of the crowds to teach something significant to his disciples. Who knows what crises Jesus has allowed or will use so that we might one day realise we have witnessed a miracle of Jesus' abundant compassion? When we appreciate God's character, we can trust his actions.

Finally, remember how the crowds ate and were satisfied without even knowing how their needs were being miraculously met? I would suggest that while we're often focused on our seemingly unanswered prayers, Jesus is miraculously meeting needs we are unaware of. Perhaps the unanswered prayer is meeting a need we cannot yet understand. God's action may be perplexing, but when you recognise his true character in Jesus, it is clear that he is far from stingy.

The headquarters of all provision

Now if we come back to the disciples, remember how Jesus asked them to feed the crowd? Jesus' identity as the generous God changes how we understand the request. The disciples would never have been able to feed all those people. These guys couldn't afford to be generous, because they had very limited resources with which to meet an almost unlimited need. Jesus created the crisis by asking the disciples to feed the crowd, not to scold them for not having the ability to feed thousands, but to highlight for them that their provision didn't need to come from themselves.

If you have ever felt the pressure of Jesus' expectations, reasonable or not, this is important to hear. If you've ever identified with the disciples' ploy to get rid of the crowds if only to be able to rest, then this story has something for you. How much pressure do you feel to live up to the life Jesus calls you to? To be kind and loving? To be gentle and honest? To serve and give? To be generous and hopeful? To tell people the good news of Jesus? To do extraordinary things that change the world? The pressure can seem unreasonable and unbearable. You can't be the person you're meant to be. Send the people away! Leave me alone! I'm not qualified for this!

Some people respond to this pressure by working harder and harder, by doing everything they can to meet the demands themselves. Others look at the demands and either put in only a half-hearted effort or don't bother at all. But neither of these options work. And both of them miss the point of what Jesus was trying to teach his disciples. Jesus didn't expect the disciples to feed all those people on their own, and he doesn't expect you to achieve all the things he asks of you either. But if Jesus is the one who is doing the providing, if he is empowering you to live for him, then you have infinite resources and you can afford to be generous, to take risks, and to rely on Jesus to provide what you need.

I am a simple man of simple loves. My tastes are not expensive (except if I get to fly first class one day, that may all change). Luxury for me is movies, potatoes, food court food, and Coca-Cola. I am well known for my love of Coca-Cola. Growing up I was never allowed to drink Coke, which meant it was scarce resource in my house. I had to drink all my Coke at parties or my grandparents' place. Anywhere I found Coke, I would drink it.

Now that I'm older and can buy myself Coke whenever I want, I still treat it like it's a scarce resource. There is never quite enough Coke. My wife likes to steal my Coke when we go to McDonald's. She will get a medium Coke, and I'll get a large. She'll finish her drink then drink some of mine. I pretend I don't mind, because she's my wife, but still I'm upset, because Coke is a scarce resource. I'll say, 'Why didn't you just get a large?', to which she'll respond, 'I didn't want a large. I wanted a medium and two sips of yours.'

There was one day when Coke was not a scarce commodity in my life. That was when I visited my friend who worked at Coca-Cola's Australian headquarters. He took me on a tour of the office, and there were Coke fridges everywhere. If you wanted a Coke, you were able to just grab one. As much Coke as you wanted, whenever you wanted. What a place to work! I've worked for a lot of churches, and all we get for free are Bibles and leftover morning tea. My friend asked me if I wanted a Coke. He wasn't stingy; he didn't need to be. He offered to give me multiple Cokes. He could give me as many as I wanted, because he had a virtually unlimited supply! In the end I took just one bottle, then we headed off to lunch. I didn't want to be greedy. I didn't want to be the guy that walked out with twenty bottles of Coke. But if I wanted it, I could have had it.

Jesus is in the headquarters of all provision. Anything and everything you need is his. Which means you have the chance for radical generosity. You don't need to be stingy with your time, your money, your energy, or your resources. You don't have to wonder how you will be faithful to Jesus. Jesus can take whatever resources you have and make them enough, because it's not about what *you* have but what *he* has.

This doesn't mean that you shouldn't spend time to retreat, rest, and renew (as Jesus was taking his disciples to do in this story). Sabbath and rest are big parts of God's desire for his people. What it means is that you aren't required to find the resources within yourself to meet the challenges Jesus places before you, whether they be loving your family, being patient with your friends, sharing the good news with others, embarking on some new ministry, or resisting sin. Jesus has everything you need and more.

Wouldn't it be amazing if, as disciples of Jesus, we were known for our generosity? Not just with our money and possessions, but with our time, our friendships, our words, our energy, our communities, ourselves. Too often we behave like the disciples, thinking we have only a finite supply of resources we must protect. We look for excuses to turn people away, not out of malice but believing we don't have what it takes. But God is not stingy. We have a God who gave himself, all of himself, in a very unreasonable act of self-sacrifice, so that we might receive every spiritual blessing in him. If he's called you to follow him, he'll give you all you need, and more, to see it through.

4

PETER SINKS

Jesus and Peter Walk on Water
Matthew 14:22-34

The sun was shining, people all around me were screaming, I was nine storeys above the ground hanging on for dear life, and the thought occurred to me, 'I did not think this through.'

Before you get too distressed on my behalf, I was at Dreamworld, a theme park on Australia's Gold Coast, and nine storeys above the ground was where I intended to be. Sort of.

I had gone to the theme park with a friend, full of excitement. I had not been to a theme park as a full-grown adult before. The last time I'd been to one, I was fourteen years old and scared of half the rides. This time, I determined I would not be afraid. I would throw myself into everything. I was an adult; I could drive a car, pay taxes, and have boring conversations about politics – I would not be scared of some perfectly safe ride. So I decided that that day I would ride anything and everything.

As we entered the park, the first ride we encountered was innocently named 'The Claw'. The ride had a circle of outward facing seats, attached to a swinging pendulum arm. The seats would rotate slowly while the arm swung from side to side. On first inspection, it looked somewhat like a swinging merry-go-round that you might find in a children's park. A nice, gentle way to ease ourselves into a day of rides.

Turns out, the ride was not gentle or nice. The ride swings you at speeds of up to 75 kilometres per hour while your seats spin like some kind of deranged carousel. As we flew up towards the sky, 27 metres into the air, I felt my kidneys trailing a few seconds behind. Then, just as they had caught up while hanging upside down at the zenith of the upswing, we went hurtling back towards the earth, this time with my stomach and intestines trying to exit via my throat. This was not how I thought it would be. I held on for dear life, wondering what I'd gotten into, saying to myself, 'I did not think this through.'

'The Claw' taught me that despite my initial bravado, I was not as brave or as capable as I thought. That day, even the *Kung Fu Panda* ride scared me a little bit. I needed to do a better job of thinking things through.

Water walking

I wonder if my encounter with 'The Claw' reminds you of times in your life when you've found yourself in a situation when the thought running through your mind is, 'I did not think this through'? It's that feeling you had as a kid when you managed to get your head stuck in a chair, or when you were a bit older and you started dating someone because they liked you, only to discover they were the kind of person who collects your toenail clippings as mementos of your love. You didn't think things through.

I suspect Peter had a similar thought when he found himself standing on the sea while the water churned beneath his feet and the wind billowed around his body. Humans are not meant to have the ability to stand on water. What had he got himself into? He didn't think it through.

How did Peter get there? That's the story we're here for, isn't it? After Jesus' amazing feeding of 20,000-ish people, he sent his disciples away in a boat on the lake, while he climbed up on a mountainside to pray (Matthew 14:22–23). But the disciples made slow progress as they headed across the water because the wind was against them. In fact, they took almost the entire night to travel a few measly kilometres (vv. 24–25).

The disciples probably regretted getting into that boat. They could have stayed on the shore, set up camp, and had a lovely meal of leftover multiplied bread, but there they were in the boat straining against the oars for hours in the cold, dark night. They were doing exactly what Jesus asked of them, and it was no fun at all. I bet some of them wished they'd thought things through a little more.

Sometimes obeying Jesus gets you into tough situations. Often the easiest option is just to do whatever you want, because what is right and what is easy are rarely the same thing. This is worth remembering. Sometimes, merely because something is hard, we think it's wrong. We're tempted to give up because it's all too much. But don't let how you feel about something trick you into believing that's the truth of the matter. Despite how it may have felt to the disciples, they were exactly where Jesus wanted them to be. And no matter how you're feeling, or how hard things are, if you're obeying Jesus, you're exactly where you should be.

Why did Jesus want them there? He had some plans up his sleeve. See what happens next: 'Shortly before dawn Jesus went out to them, walking on the lake' (v. 25).

Now, if you've grown up in church, or you're very familiar with the stories of the Bible, this may not seem remarkable to you. But read that verse again: 'Shortly before dawn Jesus went out to them, walking on the lake.'

JESUS WAS WALKING ON WATER!

This is not the type of thing that happens every day. In fact, as far as we know, it only happened on one day ever, and even that is almost beyond belief. People don't just walk on water. If I manage to stay afloat in water, I'm pretty impressed with myself, but there was Jesus having a stroll on the lake as if he was in his local park. That is very, very impressive.

Some people have found this so unbelievable that they suggest it didn't happen at all. Dubious Bible scholars have suggested that the story of Jesus walking on the water has been made up. Some suggest that he wasn't walking on water but on submerged stones, which the strong winds had uncovered enough to make accessible to anyone rambling across the lake that evening.[22] Which seems odd, because the disciples, some of whom, as we know, were very experienced fishermen who grew up fishing on that lake, would not have been sailing near submerged stones. That's asking for trouble. One of the first things they would have been taught by their fathers would have been to stay away from the stones.

Others posit that perhaps this was a translation error and Jesus wasn't walking on the lake, he was walking beside the lake.[23] I guess a translation error could happen, but I don't know why anyone would have thought that would make a good Bible story: 'Shortly before dawn Jesus went walking beside the lake.'

---

22. I probably need a reference for this claim, but I found it when preparing to preach on Jesus walking on water back in the mid-2000s, and I haven't been able to find it since. You'll just have to believe me that I didn't make it up. Don't quote this in your academic writing because you'll get in trouble. In fact, it's probably safest not to quote anything I say in academic writing. Also, how good is the word 'ramble' for walking? I heard it used in a podcast about people who would go for walks across the English countryside, and I thought I should use it more, so here it is in this book.

23. I do have a reference for this one. William Barclay, *The Gospel of John, Volume One – Chapters 1 to 7* (Edinburgh: Saint Andrew Press, 1975), 208.

Hallelujah! Amen! Praise the Lord! Jesus walked beside the lake.

What a boring story.

At Florida State University, one professor proposed that there is a phenomenon that occurs once every thousand years, when the conditions are just right, that leads to patches of ice forming on the lake.[24] So perhaps, he suggests, Jesus was walking on ice – like Disney on Ice, but with Jesus instead of Mickey. This is an interesting idea, but what are the chances that the day Jesus fed 20,000-ish people also happened to be the same day that this ice phenomenon happened, and Jesus managed to captain his ice patch out to the disciples' boat while they strained at the oars? I know the professor was attempting to solve the problem of the believability of the water walking, but it seems almost as unbelievable.

The point of all this is that it's a miracle. Jesus either did or didn't walk on the water, but if he did (which I believe he did), he did it not because of some strange phenomenon or trick of light, but because he is God himself. Jesus was once again demonstrating his identity to his disciples. Earlier, he fed all those people, showing the disciples that he is God who provides for his people in the wilderness. In this story, he was showing them he is God 'who [makes] a way through the sea, a path through the mighty waters' (Isaiah 43:16). Jesus came to his people in their distress. Just like in Exodus when

---

24. This one I also have a reference for. Libby Fairhurst, 'Jesus walked on ice, says study led by FSU scientist', *Florida State University News*. https://www.fsu.edu/news/2006/04/04/ice.walk/

God saved his people from slavery in Egypt by leading them through the parting of the sea and feeding them in the wilderness, Jesus came to the disciples in their time of need. This was giving them a foretaste of when he would meet humanity's deepest need and set all his people free from the oldest, deepest form of slavery – slavery to Satan, sin, and death. The water walking was not just a fancy trick; it was a sign of Jesus' identity and mission.

Did the disciples figure it out? Did they realise they were witnessing a new exodus? Did they welcome Jesus with cheers and relief, reflecting on the deep significance of what they had just witnessed?

Nah. They screamed. 'When the disciples saw him walking on the lake, they were terrified. "It's a ghost," they said, and cried out in fear' (Matthew 14:26).

That's actually a rather reasonable response, if you ask me. If you saw a shadowy figure coming out of the darkness across the waters towards you, you wouldn't think, 'Oh look, it's my good mate Jesus!' You'd think, 'Here is the ghost of some drowned mariner come to drag me to a watery grave.' The disciples' response makes total sense. Water walking was a totally new category of skills that Jesus demonstrated. So Jesus had to calm them down by responding, 'Take courage! It is I. Don't be afraid' (v. 27).

Peter's test

Peter still seemed unconvinced, so he devised a test: 'Lord, if it's you... tell me to come to you on the water' (v. 28). This is an odd test. Why would Peter walking on water prove Jesus' identity? That's a logical leap that I wouldn't make. 'Lord, if it's you, tell me my favourite flavour Doritos' seems more my speed. But props to Peter for his quick thinking because, while Jesus would have just responded to me, 'Nacho cheese', to Peter he said, 'Come', and Peter hopped out of the boat and literally walked on water.

What a magnificent moment: Peter walking on the water towards Jesus. What did it feel like? Was the water soft under his feet? Did it feel like walking on a pillow? Or was it hard like concrete? Was it cold? Did it feel wet? Did Peter walk right on top of the water, or did he sink a little so that the water lapped over his feet? Did he walk up and down over the waves, or through them? How does one keep their balance when walking on a shifting surface like waves? So many questions! I must remember to ask Peter when I meet him in the new creation.[25]

Peter probably wasn't thinking about most of those things. He was likely just enjoying himself. Walking on water seems pretty fun. But soon everything went wrong: 'But when he saw the wind, he was afraid and, beginning to sink, cried out, "Lord, save me!"' (v. 30).

Peter looked at what he was up against – a storm, nature, and physics, not to mention possible sharks or the kraken – and it's like he suddenly realised what he was actually doing and how improbable his situation.

---

25. I probably will not be the first person to have asked Peter this question. There's a good chance he'll just refer me to the FAQ section of his website. There are only so many times you can have the same conversation, even if you've got a spare eternity.

All the worries of reality collapsed upon him, and it was no longer about just walking out to Jesus but all the things that seem bigger than Jesus' ability to keep him afloat. He began to sink.

The irony is that the only reason why he was there in the first place was because Jesus allowed him to do the impossible. The wind and the waves had no bearing on Peter's safety. It was all Jesus.

My parents have told me a story of when I was a small boy and they took me to the fireworks for the first time. For days leading up to the event, I was so excited that I told everyone I met about my upcoming trip to see fireworks. When the night arrived, I hopped in the car with my family, chattering excitedly about what promised to be a spectacular event. We went to the park to watch the fireworks, and my dad held me as we waited for the show to begin. Unfortunately, I didn't see any of it. As soon as the first firework exploded, I buried my head in my father's shoulder and refused to look, terrified by the noises. I missed the whole show.

While I was scared by the fireworks, I had no reason to be afraid. I was with my dad. He would not let anything happen to me. I was safe because my father wouldn't take me any place he couldn't look after me.

Peter was scared by the wind and the waves and was distracted by them, but that wasn't what he needed to focus on. Peter didn't need to be scared if he was with Jesus. It was Jesus who was keeping him safe and afloat.

Peter cried out, 'Lord, save me,' but did Peter need saving at that moment? Probably not. Jesus wouldn't let him drown. But calling out to Jesus was necessary for Peter. He needed to know it was always Jesus who kept him safe. The wind and the waves were no match for Jesus: 'Immediately Jesus reached out his hand and caught him. "You of little faith," he said, "why did you doubt?"' (v. 31).

As soon as Peter called, Jesus caught him. I like to imagine they walked back to the boat, hand in hand, as Jesus gently chided Peter for his lack of faith, probably with a smile on his face. I assume Jesus wasn't too upset with him – after all, Peter did climb out of a boat onto water.

Verses 32–33 say, 'And when they climbed into the boat, the wind died down. Then those who were in the boat worshiped him, saying, "Truly you are the Son of God."' Does this mean the disciples had finally figured out who Jesus was? I reckon they had figured out a little more of who Jesus was, but as we'll continue to discover, they hadn't got him all sorted. They would keep figuring Jesus out, even after he left them. That may seem discouraging, but as someone who worships Jesus and is also still trying to figure him out (he is God after all, there is a lot to figure out), I'm pleased that I can worship Jesus without having to have all my questions answered.

You don't have what it takes

As we reflect on this story, we may be tempted to laugh at Peter for jumping out of the boat, only to sink when he saw the wind and waves. Peter was impulsive, and he got distracted by the extreme weather, but he also walked on top of a sizeable amount of liquid, so in my book (and this is my book), he was doing pretty well. All the other disciples stayed in the boat thinking about Doritos. Not only did Peter get to experience walking on water, he also got to experience Jesus taking hold of him and rescuing him when he cried out. None of the other disciples experienced Jesus like that.

When you follow Jesus, are you more like Peter or more like the remaining disciples? Perhaps, like Peter, you rush into things without thinking them through and find you're in way over your head. Or maybe, like the rest of the disciples, you don't take enough risks – maybe you overthink things too much. Are you being obedient? Are you going where you've been called? Are you following your own desires or God's leading? Is God pleased with you? If you're an over-thinker, sometimes you may need to follow Peter's example and just go for it, knowing that Jesus will be there for you. There is a time for questions and assessing all the things that could go wrong, but there is also a time when you need to act. Whether you're an under-thinker or an over-thinker, your job is to do what Jesus asks, go where he calls, and trust him to take care of the rest.

Jesus doesn't need us to have everything figured out. Jesus wants us to obey him and to take risks for him. Sometimes, as we obey him, the challenges will seem overwhelming. Your wind and waves could come in the form of your friends' opinions of your choices, or their mockery of your beliefs. They could come in the form of your family not understanding why you're choosing a course of study that will allow you to better serve God's kingdom rather than following their ambitions for you. The wind and waves may come by choosing to hold fast to what the Bible teaches rather than giving in to what society says is 'correct'. As you face these winds and waves, you could feel like the disciples: straining against the oars, making no progress. Or you may feel like Peter;:sinking, unable to keep yourself afloat. You may feel as if you don't have what it takes to stay faithful to Jesus when everything seems to be against you.

Let me tell you a hard truth: you don't have what it takes. You can't outlast the wind and waves. You can't walk on water. You can't obey Jesus. You can't achieve the things he calls you to. But *he* can. And he never calls you to be a disciple alone. He doesn't say, 'Go be my disciple. I'll meet you at the end and you can tell me how you went.' No, when he calls you to follow him, he never leaves you alone. He comes to you in your distress. He takes hold of you in your weakness and sin and lifts you up. He is God who has made a way to be with you. He didn't just make a way across the waters, but he made a way through death and back so he might rescue you from sin and death and empower you to live for him. Jesus came to earth and went to the cross, to death, and to new life, so you would be his. That is the kind of commitment that you can rely on, whatever wind and waves you are experiencing.

As you embark on each new step in your journey of following Jesus, think it through. Do you have what you need to keep following Jesus? The answer is, yes, you do. If you trust in Jesus, you have him with you through his Spirit. He'll be with you as you struggle through the wind and waves. If you find yourself sinking, cry out to him – he'll lift you up. With him, I promise, you will make it through. And from time to time, you may even find yourself walking on water.[26]

---

26. I hate to spoil such an inspiring ending with a footnote, but you know I don't literally mean you'll walk on water. It's a metaphor for achieving great things for Jesus. I mean, if Jesus decides to empower you to walk on water, that's totally his prerogative, but as far as I know only two people have ever done it.

5

'IT'S NOT ABOUT THE BREAD'

The Yeast of Herod and the Pharisees
Mark 8:1–21

Recently, my wife had a job interview for a role she was interested in. However, before the interview, she needed to sit an exam at her university. She asked me to meet her at uni and bring her a dress that she could get changed into for the job interview. She didn't want to carry the outfit with her all morning, so it was my job to deliver the dress and keep it crease-free. We decided we would also have lunch when I came to see her. Before she left, she reminded me, 'Don't forget the dress.' All throughout the day I said to myself, 'Don't forget the dress.' I had the dress hanging by the front door so that when I left, I wouldn't forget it.

When it was time, I drove to her uni. We met and ate lunch together. It was a lovely little middle of the day lunch date. But after lunch when I went to give her the dress that should have been hanging in the car, I discovered I had forgotten it! Typical me. I don't know how much more I could have done to make sure I didn't forget the dress.[27] Some tasks are just too hard for folks like me.

In this story in Mark 8, we see the disciples display a seemingly impossible amount of thick-headedness. The story begins as we find the disciples with Jesus, not in Jewish territory anymore, but, as usual, there was a crowd around Jesus wanting to hear his teaching. There were 4,000 people this time. After days of teaching, Jesus was concerned with how hungry all the people must have been. He turned to the disciples and said, 'I have compassion for these people; they have already been with me three days and have nothing to eat. If I send them home hungry, they will collapse on the way, because some of them have come a long distance' (vv. 2–3).

Now, you would think if Jesus presented a problem like this to the disciples that they could have remembered back to that other time, not that long ago, when they were with an even larger crowd that they needed to feed, and Jesus fed them all with barely any food. So when

---

27. Happily, I raced home while she did her make-up and got the dress. I got it back to her in time for her to get changed for the interview and I'm pleased to report that she got the job. I'm also pleased to report that she was graciously calm the whole time and I didn't get in trouble at all for my stupid mistake, which I certainly deserved.

Jesus mentioned that this crowd was hungry, the disciples should have realised that the answer was literally staring them right in the face – blinking, breathing, and talking.

Instead, the disciples replied, 'But where in this remote place can anyone get enough bread to feed them?' (v. 4). What a brilliant question. Where could anyone get enough bread? I don't know, I'm just putting it out there – Jesus, perhaps? This wasn't really a theoretical, untested solution, was it?

To be fair, it was Jesus presenting the problem, so perhaps they assumed that if Jesus was asking, he might not have a solution. Perhaps they thought his power had run out, or he couldn't do feeding miracles outside of his home territory. Who knows?

However, Jesus didn't mess around with rebuking the disciples when they didn't understand. He just got on with feeding all those people. He asked the disciples how much bread they had, and they found seven loaves. They were also able to find some fish. So Jesus had the disciples distribute it, and just like before, everyone ate and was satisfied. At the end, seven basketfuls were left over. And again, the disciples hopped in the boat to sail to the region of Dalmanutha. Unfortunately, despite the abundance of leftovers, they only took one loaf with them.[28]

---

28. This oversight could be one of the most egregious mistakes of the disciples in my opinion. Leftovers are one of my favourite things in life. There are many meals that get better a day or two after they've been cooked. What joy it is to have last night's butter chicken for lunch when everyone else is eating boring sandwiches! This is why one of my favourite verses in the Bible is Psalm 17:14 –

Asking for a sign

When they arrived at their destination, like a bunch of seagulls sensing some chips, out came the local Pharisees with a test for Jesus. I assume, after some of Jesus' public arguments with the Pharisees (see Mark 7:1–23 for a particularly juicy one) that they were keen to show their resolve. They asked him for a sign from heaven. This might seem like a weird request. Jesus had just fed thousands of people – twice – and walked on water. You would think they had received enough signs. But they probably didn't know that the feeding miracles were miracles; they just thought they were conventional mass feedings. And I assume the story of Jesus walking on water hadn't reached the Pharisees yet; these were miracles designed only for the disciples to witness. Still, he had done plenty of public healings by this point. But that wasn't enough for them. In fact, sometimes the healings were the problem (see Mark 3:1–6)! They wanted Jesus to prove he was not just some cheap conjurer of tricks, but God's Messiah. They wanted proof that God endorsed Jesus. Perhaps Jesus could have made himself glow, called down fire on someone, rapped Alphabet Aerobics, or something equally impressive.

Instead of giving them a sign, Jesus sighed deeply. Which I guess was a sign, though not from heaven, just a sign that these people completely frustrated him. 'Why does this generation ask for a sign? Truly I tell you, no sign will be given to it' (v. 12). In Matthew's account,

---

'May there be leftovers.' So you can understand why I feel like it is almost a crime to leave so many baskets of miracle bread behind.

Jesus said, 'A wicked and adulterous generation asks for a sign! But none will be given it except the sign of the prophet Jonah. For as Jonah was three days and three nights in the belly of a huge fish, so the Son of Man will be three days and three nights in the heart of the earth' (Matthew 12:39–40). Jesus would give them a sign: it would be his death and resurrection, but the Pharisees would not recognise it for what it was. No number of signs would satisfy people who refused to see.

I have had a few people tell me that for them to become a Christian, God would need to send them a sign. Some of them tell me they have asked for a sign from God to prove that he is real, which they didn't receive, so they aren't Christians. This seems reasonable on the surface – it's not like it costs God anything to throw a few lightning bolts or personalised rainbows around. But the premise is problematic. If the onus is on God to prove himself to us, then he becomes our servant. God has given us plenty of proof of himself, if only we would look for it (Romans 1:20); he's not required to provide a sign every time we demand one.

Imagine what would happen if I demanded my wife regularly prove that she loves me. Every few days she'd be baking me a cake, going out to buy me Maccas late at night, or announcing her love for me in some sappy Instagram post. Now, if she does any of those things without me demanding it, I'm going to feel very loved. But if she does them because I demand it, I've distorted our relationship, and I suspect I won't trust the signs, anyway. I'll always need more proof.

Also, you can see all the signs and still not believe. Judas saw all Jesus' miracles right until he betrayed him. I know people who have witnessed amazing miracles and still choose not to follow Jesus. Be careful of demanding God prove himself to you. Even if he did, you probably wouldn't be satisfied, anyway.

There is another time in the Bible when someone asks Jesus for some assurance of his identity, and he gives it. John the Baptist (Jesus' cousin, whom we discussed in Chapter 1) had been thrown in prison. There, he began to doubt if Jesus really was who he said he was, so he sent his own disciples to Jesus to ask him if he really was the Messiah, or should they expect someone else. Jesus didn't say to him, 'I tell you, no sign will be given to you.' Jesus instead responded by saying, 'Go back and report to John what you hear and see: the blind receive sight, the lame walk, those who have leprosy are cleansed, the deaf hear, the dead are raised, and the good news is proclaimed to the poor. Blessed is anyone who does not stumble on account of me' (Matthew 11:4–6). Jesus didn't do an amazing miracle for John's disciples, but he pointed to his works as a sign that he really was the one who John had been proclaiming.

The difference in these two interactions was that while the Pharisees demanded a sign from Jesus so that he might prove himself to them, John asked as one who was committed to Jesus, but was having a crisis of faith. John didn't demand a sign, he just asked Jesus if he really was who he said he was. Jesus responded not by refusing proof, or rebuking John for his lack of faith, but by encouraging him to look at what he had been doing: the very work that should have accompanied God's Messiah.

There are always exceptions to every rule, and you may be able to think of stories where people have asked for signs and God has given them. I don't want to take anything away from those experiences. There is nothing wrong with genuinely asking for a sign. The problem is in the demand. God can and does give signs, because he is a God of grace. Jesus was gracious in his response to John, and the signs we may get from him demonstrate his grace to us, but he owes us nothing. If you ask for a sign and get none, that doesn't mean that God doesn't exist or love you, anymore than me not answering every phone call I get is a sign that I'm unable to use a phone.

So if you just wish Jesus would prove himself to you, perhaps it's worth getting to know Jesus through the stories in the Bible, and asking him to reveal himself to you in that way, before you demand signs and proofs. I suspect if you do that, you'll find you get to know Jesus without needing to demand anything of him, and if you do get some kind of sign, what an excellent, unnecessary gift from him to you.

Bread and yeast

After Jesus refused the Pharisees a sign, Mark writes this: 'Then he left them, got back into the boat and crossed to the other side' (8:13).

Let's just recap what happened there. Jesus and the disciples arrived in the region of Dalmanutha, they got out of the boat, the Pharisees asked for a sign, Jesus sighed and told them they weren't getting a sign, then they got back in the boat and headed back across the lake. It feels kind of like those family blow-ups where Mum, Dad, and the kids arrive at Grandma and Grandpa's house. Grandpa says something offensive about Mum as soon as they arrive, so Dad, defending Mum's honour, makes the family get back in the car, and they go home.

As they're leaving, Dad turns around to the kids and says, 'Promise me if you get married you won't let anyone talk about your husband or wife the way your grandfather just talked about your mother.' To which the kids dutifully reply, 'Okay,' while having no idea what is going on. This is kind of what Jesus did. As they were in the boat, Jesus turned to the disciples and said, 'Be careful... Watch out for the yeast of the Pharisees and that of Herod' (v. 15).

Jesus was clearly referring to the conversation he'd just had with the Pharisees, but the disciples did not understand what he was talking about. They thought he was upset because they only had one loaf of bread with them in the boat. Can you imagine that conversation among the disciples?

> Peter: Jesus, are you upset that we didn't bring any bread? Thomas, I told you to bring some bread.

> Thomas: I thought Andrew was going to do it, he was closest to the baskets.

Andrew: Don't look at me, I found the baskets to collect the bread, it shouldn't be my responsibility to put them in the boat as well.

Peter: Didn't anyone think of bringing some for a snack? There were seven basketfuls.

Judas: Seven! How could you let seven baskets of perfectly good bread go to waste!

Jesus: Guys! It's not about the bread!

Jesus clearly wasn't worried about the bread. It seems a little crazy to me that the disciples would even think Jesus was worried about literal bread. He obviously had some serious skills in bread production, but it seems the disciples forgot this fact, which is why the following conversation ensued:

'Why are you talking about having no bread? Do you still not see or understand? Are your hearts hardened? Do you have eyes but fail to see, and ears but fail to hear? And don't you remember? When I broke the five loaves for the five thousand, how many basketfuls of pieces did you pick up?'

'Twelve,' they replied.

'And when I broke the seven loaves for the four thousand, how many basketfuls of pieces did you pick up?'

93

> They answered, 'Seven.'
>
> He said to them, 'Do you still not understand?' (vv. 17–21)

Jesus was understandably frustrated that the disciples couldn't get their heads around the fact that he was not like everyone else. He wasn't concerned with the daily realities of where to get food. Not that he didn't need food, but he trusted his Father to provide. If he trusted his Father, then his disciples could trust him. Jesus didn't worry that they would starve to death. He was much more concerned with the disciples' spiritual well-being: a much bigger danger for the disciples was that they might be infected by the 'yeast' of the Pharisees and Herod.

You would think from what Jesus said that the Pharisees and Herod might have been in cahoots, but actually they were not similar at all. The Pharisees were a conservative religious sect, and Herod was a regional ruler propped up by Rome. What they had in common, however, was that both wouldn't believe in Jesus and his mission, and eventually both would be instrumental in his death.

Because the Pharisees wouldn't acknowledge him as the promised Messiah, Jesus seemed to be concerned that the same disbelief seen in the Pharisees and Herod (who had recently killed John the Baptist) could work its way into the attitudes of the disciples. They clearly weren't getting their heads around who Jesus was. They had eyes that had witnessed Jesus do amazing things, had ears that listened to his authoritative teaching, but none of those things had helped them truly understand who Jesus was. If they had, they wouldn't have worried about the bread.

As dull as the disciples seem to be here, I totally get where they're coming from. While Jesus is talking about spiritual things, they're stuck on the physical things – they're worried about bread. Their bread-based concerns resonate with me. So much of my life is concerned with surface-level concerns, when I should be much more concerned about what is going on spiritually. I spend much of my life concerned about money, when in my experience God has always provided more than my needs. I'm much more likely not to think about my spiritual health, or the spiritual health of those around me, or just to assume that things are going fine and will continue to be fine.

The problem with all this is that if I focus on the surface level stuff, I'll miss out on what Jesus is really doing. Jesus never actually explained what he meant by the 'yeast of the Pharisees and that of Herod' so the disciples (and the rest of us by extension) missed out on whatever important teaching Jesus offered.

I rarely feel like a very spiritual person. I heard a woman on TV describe herself as 'spiritually dumb', which resonated with me, because often that's exactly how I feel. I sit in prayer meetings and all I can think about is how long there is to go until the prayer meeting is over. When I hear that someone is sick, my first response isn't to pray for them; it's just to feel helpless. When I meet people who don't know Jesus, particularly if their life seems to be going well, it doesn't occur to me that they need Jesus, as if having good health and material wealth is a suitable substitute for knowing Jesus. I have a very bread-based life.

My father, on the other hand, does not live a very bread-based life at all. I remember as a kid we often seemed to run out of money, and my parents had to trust that God would provide – and he did. It's not that my father didn't earn much money. As far as I know, his job paid okay. It's just my father seems to have spent a lot of his life trying to avoid making a lot of money. He is aware of what wealth can do to his heart, so instead of chasing more money, my parents actively give money away. Part of the reason why, when I was growing up, they kept having no money in their bank account was because it was with a charity or in someone else's bank account who they felt needed it more.

Sometimes my father's reliance on Jesus would infuriate me. Not because we didn't have as much stuff as I wanted, but because my father insisted, and still insists, on seeking God's will in all sorts of matters. Like in Year 8, when I wanted to take the last day of the year off school because the year before only seven people in my grade had turned up. I asked my dad if I could have the day off, and he prayed about it for what seemed like months. I thought it should be a fairly straightforward decision, but my dad cared a lot more about what God wanted than what I wanted.

Even today, I can find myself in a discussion with him about what to order at a restaurant, and he'll talk about discerning the perfect will of God, and I'm not entirely sure how much he is joking. Happily for the rest of us in his family, he doesn't pray and fast for an hour before ordering a gluten-free vegetarian pad Thai.

As much as we gently tease my father about things like this, I know that his focus on Jesus has helped him to live a life of spiritual integrity. He takes doing the will of God seriously, and he doesn't just assume he knows what is right. There are few people in my life who have shown me what following Jesus looks like better than my father. For him, it's clearly not about the bread.

What is your 'bread'? What is it that distracts you from paying attention to what really matters? Is it negotiating the politics of your friendship group? Is it making sure you have the right social media presence? Is it finishing the latest video game? Is it being the best sports person you can be? For some of you, it will be things like getting good marks and making sure you do well at school or at your job. For others, it will be working on a romantic relationship. While many of these things are good and useful, they are just bread. They are not your true calling in life. Your true calling is to recognise who Jesus is and follow him obediently.

How terrible to get to the end of your life and realise you've spent your entire life focused on bread when Jesus was calling you to something much better, much more exciting.

So how do you make sure that you don't make the same mistake as the disciples? Their mistake was that they were focused on the things that didn't matter, so they risked missing out on the things that did. Their primary focus on bread wasn't at all what Jesus was concerned about. It might be useful then to assess what you spend your time thinking about and what you spend your emotional energy on. When Jesus spoke to the disciples about yeast, their first instinct was to worry about bread. Had they realised that Jesus had the bread situation covered, they could easily have dismissed that as an option and asked, 'What do you mean by the "yeast of the Pharisees and that of Herod"?' And then they would have received an answer.

If we can rest in the fact that with Jesus our most basic needs are sorted – he has done everything needed to bring us into a good relationship with God, forever – then we can have the space to focus on what matters. That is, knowing and becoming more like Jesus, and helping those around us know and become more like Jesus, too. It's not about the bread.

6

JESUS CALLS PETER SATAN

Peter's Confession and Rebuke
Matthew 16:13–28

Do you know that sinking feeling when you get in trouble? For instance, in school when the teacher caught you doing something wrong and called you on it? I don't know about you, but even though it's been many years since I was a student in school, I still get the same feelings if I think I'm in trouble. My legs feel like jelly, my hands shake, I can't talk properly, and I feel like I will cry. If you're trying to give the impression of being a nonchalant rebel, becoming a wobbly, trembly, blubbery mess doesn't really do you any favours.

I was a well-behaved kid in school, but there were a few times when I stepped outside the bounds of school law. Perhaps my most terrible act of blatant disobedience happened when I was just seven years old. How can a seven-year-old be a criminal, you ask? You just wait. My actions will shock you.

Every week in class we would have a multiplication drill. The teacher would give us a number, then we would have to figure out how to multiply that number by the numbers one to ten. My favourite weeks were the weeks we had to do the one or the ten times tables. Those were within my intellectual grasp; the others were somewhat more baffling. One afternoon, as the teacher (who I had a small crush on) was preparing us for our multiplication drill, I decided it was time to pull off a caper I had been planning for at least five minutes. Key to my plan was the fact that our desks had lids that swung up so you could store stuff inside them, which was great for sticking posters on the inside of your desk and terrible for keeping anything on your desk while you retrieved something inside it. I lifted the lid of my desk, hid my head behind it, put one hand to my mouth to create a pressurised seal through which rapidly escaping air would cause loud vibrations, and blew out to make the loudest fart noise I could – 'Ffffffffffffffffrrrrrrrrrttttttttffffffftttttttttffffftttt!' It was a majestic piece of subversive, Bansky-esq sonic art. I put the lid of my desk down, satisfied that I had just executed the prank of the century, when my teacher said, 'Tom! Outside! Now!' Why is it so difficult to be bad?

I walked out of the classroom, embarrassed to have been called out in front of all my classmates. I took a seat near the water fountains, with jelly legs and shaking hands, waiting for the beginning of the end. What would happen to me? Would I get suspended? Would I be expelled? What would my family say? Would they visit me in prison?

Needless to say, my worst fears were not realised. But I did get a dressing-down for my immature behaviour (I was seven, so I feel like immature behaviour is exactly what should have been expected from me). I was allowed to go back into the classroom, and I wandered in feeling not like a returning hero but like a silly kid who had been caught in front of all his friends doing a silly thing.

This chapter, we're looking at a time when Peter got himself into a very public spot of bother. I wonder if he felt the same way that I did? He didn't make any fart noises or get told off by his beloved Year 2 teacher, but he did get publicly rebuked for something that is arguably more significant than the rapid expulsion of air between mouth, cheek, and hand.

Peter's triumph

It all began when Jesus and his disciples rocked up to some villages near Caesarea Philippi in the north of Israel. Jesus turned to his disciples and asked them, 'Who do people say the Son of Man is?' (Matthew 16:13). This is the ancient equivalent of googling yourself. If I google myself, I find out I'm a British artist who paints skulls, an American journalist who has won the Pulitzer Prize, a Russian architect, and an Irish poet. I wonder if those other Tom Frenches google themselves and find me? Is that disappointing for them?

What did Jesus find in his ancient Google? The disciples told him, 'Some say John the Baptist; others say Elijah; and still others, Jeremiah or one of the prophets' (v. 14).

The disciples have their ear to the ground; they know what people are saying. Some people reckon Jesus is John the Baptist, which is probably a simple mistake to make seeing as they are cousins and they both preach. However, by this stage in the story, John the Baptist has been beheaded for preaching against King Herod's decision to sleep with his sister-in-law (Matthew 14:1–12). So it is a less easy mistake to make.

Other people reckoned Jesus was one of the ancient prophets, also come back to life. In the book of Malachi there was a prophecy that Elijah (the prophet who asked God to burn up the cows on the top of Mount Carmel) would come back before the day that God brought his justice to the earth (Malachi 4:5). Jeremiah was a prophet who wasn't particularly popular with the authorities for his prophesies of doom, and perhaps people associated the way Jesus was upsetting the authorities of his day with Jeremiah's ministry.

All these speculations about Jesus' identity seem rather far-fetched, but it's obvious that Jesus wasn't just any old guy. He had to be quite impressive for the most reasonable explanation of his identity to be that he was someone back from the dead.[29]

---

29. Okay. I don't want to be unfair to the ancients. The fact that people were saying that Jesus was dead people may not actually mean that they thought Jesus was actually those people. They may have been referring to the dead people 'as models to identify

Jesus then asked the disciples, 'Who do you say that I am?' (Matthew 16:15). Peter, who had become the unofficial spokesperson for the disciples, said what is perhaps the most insightful thing he said in the entire Gospels: 'Simon Peter answered, "You are the Messiah, the Son of the living God"' (v. 16).

Peter was saying that Jesus was the chosen one who had been long prophesied about in the Israelite Scriptures. Jesus was the King who, it was foretold, would perfectly rule God's people and restore Israel to its role as a leading nation and light to the world. Peter was harking back to the glorious days of King David and King Solomon, and looking forward to an even greater future for God's people.

Jesus liked Peter's answer: 'Blessed are you, Simon son of Jonah, for this was not revealed to you by flesh and blood, but by my Father in heaven' (v. 17).

Oh, boy! Imagine how Peter must have felt hearing those words. He'd figured it out. Other people were still fumbling about making wrong guesses about Jesus' identity, but not Peter. Peter was smart. Peter was knowledgeable. Of course, it was God who revealed it to Peter, but really, it probably felt like a team effort. God gave Peter the clues, but Peter used all his Sherlock Holmes mind palace power to deduce the truth!

Jesus continued: 'And I tell you that you are Peter, and on this rock I will build my church' (v. 18).

---

the nature of Jesus' ministry [which] need not necessarily imply their personal return.' R. T. France, *The Gospel of Matthew* (Grand Rapids: Eerdmans, 2007), 616.

A Dozen Disappointing Disciples

Hold on. What? Isn't Peter's name Peter? Why has Jesus been calling him Simon? And why is he only now calling him Peter?

Let me explain. As I touched on earlier, Peter's name was Simon. That's what his parents named him. His dad's name was Jonah, so as the son of Jonah he would have been called Simon bar Jonah, or as we might call him, Simon Jonahson. But Jesus chose to rename him Peter, so by the time they wrote the Bible everyone called him Peter, which is why we've been calling him Peter too!

So why did Jesus call Simon, Peter? The name Peter means 'Rock' or 'Rocky'. Jesus was essentially naming him Simon 'The Rock' Jonahson, which is eerily similar to Dwayne 'The Rock' Johnson. I'm not saying that there is necessarily a connection there, but someone should really look into it.

Aside from Jesus' subtle prophecy about The People's Champ, Jesus was making a pun with Peter's new name. Peter had figured out who Jesus truly was, and Jesus was affirming that on 'this rock' he would build his church. There has been a lot of discussion about this verse over the years, by people a lot smarter than I am, but it seems to me that Jesus was telling Peter that just as he had become a spokesperson for the Twelve, so he would be the leader of Jesus' church after Jesus departed. It is on the leadership of Peter, to whom God had revealed the truth of his Son, that Jesus would establish his church.[30]

---

30. Some of you are wondering if I'm affirming that Peter was the first Catholic pope, and all subsequent popes are in direct succession to Peter. With apologies to my Catholic friends, I'm not. I'm only saying

But that's not all. Look at the whole of what Jesus said: 'And I tell you that you are Peter, and on this rock I will build my church, and the gates of Hades will not overcome it. I will give you the keys of the kingdom of heaven; whatever you bind on earth will be bound in heaven, and whatever you loose on earth will be loosed in heaven' (vv. 17–18).

This church that Jesus was building wasn't going to be stopped, not even by death. And guess who would oversee the whole thing, leading it with heavenly authority? Simon 'The Rock' Jonahson.

If Peter was feeling good before, he was probably feeling even better after this. Simon was now a rock, the rock on which Jesus would establish his gathered people! They once made me a VIP at my local cinema because I went so much, and that felt pretty darn good. Peter was to become a VIP of Jesus' people – he must have felt amazing. That's much more impressive than my thing (but Peter didn't get free popcorn refills like I did, so I've got that at least). And it might just be Peter's inflated feelings of self-importance about Jesus' pronouncements that led directly to what happened next.

Peter's disgrace

After Jesus had established with his disciples who he was, we're told that he began teaching them about what he would have to endure: 'From that time on Jesus began

that Peter was chosen by Jesus to be the foundational leader of the church, I don't think Jesus is making any statement here about anyone who might come after Peter in terms of church leadership.

to explain to his disciples that he must go to Jerusalem and suffer many things at the hands of the elders, the chief priests and the teachers of the law, and that he must be killed and on the third day be raised to life' (v. 21).

Jesus wouldn't be the Messiah everyone expected. He wasn't about to lead an army into Jerusalem, kick out the Romans, and establish his kingdom. He was going to Jerusalem where he would be tortured and killed, only to rise to new life. That was the true lot of the Messiah. Peter, however, didn't like this idea: 'Peter took him aside and began to rebuke him. "Never, Lord!" he said. "This shall never happen to you!"' (v. 22).

Peter, the great and wise Peter who had just figured out Jesus' true identity, heard Jesus' warnings about what was to come and decided that Jesus had got it all wrong.

So Peter pulled him aside and began to rebuke him. 'What are you talking about, Jesus? Messiahs don't die. You've got to stop with all this negative talk and get your head in the game. Do you think we're following you just so you can go get killed? That's not how this happens. You should read your Bible, Jesus!'

Peter was Petersplaining to the Messiah what the Messiah is meant to do. But Jesus wasn't having any of it: 'Jesus turned and said to Peter, "Get behind me, Satan! You are a stumbling-block to me; you do not have in mind the concerns of God, but merely human concerns"' (v. 23).

Poor old Peter. He was having such a good day, then Jesus called him Satan. Isn't that always the way? Life seems to be going really well, and then the Lord of the Universe calls you the Lord of Evil.

Why would Jesus do this? Wasn't he meant to be a nice guy? Jesus normally was nice to people. He said some harsh things to the Pharisees, and one time he called some people who were listening to his teaching children of the devil (John 8:44). But do you know what's worse than being called a child of Satan? Being called Satan himself. I don't know, but it just seems very impolite to call someone the Dark Lord.

The problem is that when Peter rebuked Jesus, he was rebuking him for saying that he was going to be arrested and killed. Though it didn't fit with Peter's ideas about the Messiah, Jesus knew that going to the cross was the only way to achieve what he set out to achieve. To attempt to dissuade Jesus from the cross was the work of Satan.

When Satan tempts us, he doesn't do it with things we don't like or that seem impossible. He's not stupid. Satan never whispers in your ear, 'Hey, see that hammer? Why don't you pick it up and hit yourself in the head with it?'[31] Because you'll just say, 'No. That would hurt.' Also, Satan has never tempted me to start a nuclear war, because that's an impossibility. That would be a waste of

---

31. I know someone is reading this saying, 'What about mental illness?' or, 'What about that kid who was possessed by a demon and it kept throwing him into a fire?' Stop with your 'whatabouts'. I'm not talking about mental illness or demon possession. Of course, we both know there are exceptions to everything, but I think you understand my point.

energy for Satan. Instead, Satan tempts us with things we want, and things that seem possible.

In Matthew 4 we read how Satan tempted Jesus in the desert. The temptations were things that Jesus wanted. Satan tempted Jesus by showing him all the kingdoms of the world and saying, 'All this I will give you... if you will bow down and worship me' (v. 9). This was a temptation for Jesus to inherit his kingdom without having to die on the cross. I can imagine that would be extremely tempting. Jesus didn't want to die. That was obvious when he was praying to his Father in the Garden of Gethsemane just before he was to be arrested and executed. Jesus asked God to not have to go to the cross. However, despite his feelings, he submitted himself to God's will (Matthew 26:42). You can be sure that Satan knew that Jesus didn't want to die. If he could tempt him not to achieve his mission, he would win!

So, when Peter rebuked Jesus for all his crazy talk about suffering and death, he was literally being a mouthpiece for Satan. Jesus knew how much rested on his mission to the cross, and so he rejected Peter's words in the harshest possible terms.

Peter hadn't spent any time trying to discern God's will; he'd just heard Jesus say something he didn't agree with and got himself into a right mess. This probably wasn't a difficult trap to fall into. We too can easily become a mouthpiece for Satan when we advocate for things that go against God's will. Usually we don't intend to do this; we just fail to spend any time reflecting on what is actually right and true and go with what *feels* right and true.

A few years ago in Australia, the government sent out a survey to every voter in the country to ask if they thought same-sex marriage should be legal.[32] If the majority of people who returned the survey agreed, then the government would enact laws to make same-sex marriage legal. If the majority of people didn't agree, then legal marriage in Australia would remain only between a man and a woman.

As soon as the survey was announced, campaigns to vote yes and vote no were launched. I got worried that Christians, in an attempt to persuade others of their views, would say things that were unloving and hurt our ability to share the love of Jesus with the world.

I wrote a blog post calling for Christians to remember to be loving, regardless of how they intended to respond to the survey. Somehow, it struck a nerve and went a small amount of viral. I started receiving messages from Christians thanking me for the post. And many of them assumed they knew how I was going to respond to the survey because they knew the 'Christian' way to respond. Except that there were people who believed the true Christian position was to vote no, and others who thought it was to vote yes.

I found people on both sides of the debate had a few key Bible verses they could quote. I also found that

32. The exact wording was 'Should the law be changed to allow same-sex couples to marry?' 'Australian Marriage Law Postal Survey, 2017', https://abs.gov.au/ausstats/abs@.nsf/mf/1800.0

Christians on both sides claimed to be the most loving and the most biblical. And Christians on both sides behaved in ways that were both unloving and unbiblical. It's easy to talk about what's right while behaving in a way that is wrong.

Many Christians didn't just make their decisions for how to vote from the Bible, but from the social media they consumed, the people they were friends with, or what their gut told them. Unsurprisingly, I found the people who mostly spent time with people who supported the 'no' argument were likely to vote no, and expected me to vote no. People who spent time with others who supported the 'yes' argument were equally likely to vote yes, and expected me to vote yes.

I'm not telling you this to make an argument about the ethics of legalising same-sex marriage in Australia. I'm telling you this to illustrate how for Christians on both sides, it is easy to make assumptions about what is 'right' because they are going with the flow of their subculture rather than taking the time to search the Scriptures through the lens of Jesus' ethic of love.

I see this often in all sorts of contemporary issues. Whether it's to do with climate change, gender and sexuality, abortion, religious freedom, or something else. When we are confronted by these and other issues, we need to make sure we don't make the mistake of thinking we know what God thinks.

We're about to read about Jesus telling the disciples about the cost of following him. I would hazard a guess that if your opinion on any thorny issue does not make you uncomfortable – because it could make you an outsider with your friends or family, because it requires you to love people you don't want to love, or because it means you will have to change your mind and your behaviour – then there's a good chance you haven't yet found God's heart on the matter.

Peter would not have run into trouble if he had not waded in with his assumption about the right way for a Messiah to behave. Had he stopped, listened carefully to Jesus, felt the discomfort of his words, and then asked him to explain more, he wouldn't have made the mess he did.

So how do we make sure we don't do the same thing as Peter? I'm not implying that there is one clear, easy, biblical answer to many of the issues we may face. In fact, I'm sure that often there isn't. Some things are straightforward, but many things will require us to resist the temptation to have an opinion about every issue. We need to be able to say, 'I don't know.' We need to ask more questions, to listen more, and most importantly to spend time humbly searching God's Word for answers, asking him to help us know the right way to respond, and pay the cost of doing so.

The upside-down kingdom

Getting back to the story, after rebuking Peter, Jesus turned to the group and said this:

> Whoever wants to be my disciple must deny themselves and take up their cross and follow me. For whoever wants to save their life will

lose it, but whoever loses their life for me will find it. What good will it be for someone to gain the whole world, yet forfeit their soul? Or what can anyone give in exchange for their soul? For the Son of Man is going to come in his Father's glory with his angels, and then he will reward each person according to what they have done.

Truly I tell you, some who are standing here will not taste death before they see the Son of Man coming in his kingdom. (Matthew 16:24–28)

Peter had clearly not understood how God's kingdom works, so Jesus gave him and the disciples this teaching. The point Jesus was making is that God's kingdom is an upside-down kingdom. In his kingdom, things don't function how we might expect them to. You save your life by losing it. The King wins by dying. Following Jesus doesn't win you power and authority; it costs you your life.

When Peter declared who Jesus was, Jesus told the disciples not to tell anyone (v. 20). This wasn't because he wanted to save it to be a surprise later. He wasn't planning some magnificent Messiah reveal party. He told them not to tell anyone because before his death and resurrection, no one would understand what he was really about. Peter's rebuke of Jesus makes that pretty clear. If Peter couldn't understand it, how could anyone else? Only after the cross could the upside-down nature of Jesus' kingdom begin to be grasped – where the King is enthroned on a cross, death defeats death, and life is available to those who will give it up.

If you're serious about following Jesus and living in God's kingdom, things will not always go the way you expect them to. Like Peter, you will discover that God's agenda is not the same as yours. While we want to follow our dreams and desires, Jesus calls us to follow him, in the way of the cross, even to the point of death.

In some parts of the world, Christians risk actual, physical death for their commitment to Jesus. For many of us, however, that is not our reality. But Jesus still has the same words for us. To take up your cross means to put to death all those things in yourself that might stop you from having full allegiance to Jesus. To put to death your greed, your selfishness, your prejudice, your apathy. To replace them with love, commitment, courage, and openness in submission to King Jesus. As you do this, you turn your life upside down. You discover that Jesus' call to death is really a call to truly live. You find that you are living the way you were designed to live.

Peter made the mistake of thinking he knew what was right, without truly listening to Jesus. We too can easily make that mistake – but we don't have to. And if we're willing to humbly listen to Jesus, to assume that we don't always know what is right, to accept that perhaps what is right is the opposite of what we think it is, we can save ourselves from making the same mistake as Peter.

7

PETER WANTS TO BUILD TENTS

The Transfiguration
Mark 9:2–13

I was once at the pub with a friend. We were there for lunch and hadn't had anything to drink. After lunch, we decided it might be fun to play a game of pool. My friend was wearing a hoodie that had a large Christian fish on its back.[33]

---

33. If you're not familiar with the Christian fish, it's an ancient symbol that early Christians used to secretly identify themselves to each other in the face of persecution. These days, some Christians still use it to identify themselves, but I'm not sure why. For some reason, it used to be very popular to have one on the back of your car. Perhaps so other Christians will avoid crashing into them and crash into the non-Christian car instead.

As we began playing, three people also walked into the poolroom, two men and a woman. By the way they were behaving it was clear that if they had come to the pub for lunch, most of their lunch had been liquid. These three noticed that my friend and I were playing pool, and they asked if we wanted to play a game with them, my friend and me versus the two guys. We agreed, and the game began.

During the game, one guy noticed my friend's hoodie. 'Are you guys Christians?' he asked. My friend replied that indeed we were. This led to a lot of ribbing about our faith as we continued to play the game. At some point I remember the man shouting, 'The Christians versus the heathens! The Christians versus the heathens! Throw the Christians to the lions!'

After a few minutes of this, the man turned to me as I leant against the pool table and said, 'You don't mind me teasing you, do you?'

'No,' I replied. 'That's what you do with your friends. You tease them.'

At this, the guy spun around, grabbed me by the throat, and forced me back so I was lying on the top of the pool table. 'You think we're friends? You think we're friends?'

This turn of events was rather shocking to me. When I went to the pub for some lunch, I had not expected that I might be choked to death on a pool table. I didn't know what to do. Having no martial arts training (apart from once getting two free kung fu lessons), I didn't know how to resist a drunk pool player's choke hold. All I could think to do was to narrate the situation. Which was never going to do anyone any good, but narrate I did.

With a voice that sounded like some kind of dying puppet, I said, 'I'm being choked on a pool table,' while I looked at my friend, trying to send signals with my eyes to get him to help me. Now my friend is a rather large guy, so I thought, 'If there is anyone you want to get into a fight at the pub with, it's this guy.' My friend laid a hand gently on my assailant's shoulder, and the guy took one look at him and immediately removed his hand from my throat.

'Of course we're friends, mate! But I scared ya, didn't I?'

'Ha! What excellent friends we are!'

We finished our game and got out of there pretty quickly.

There are some people who know exactly what to do in a crisis. My friend is one of them. I am not. Narrating your own death, while perhaps amusing, doesn't really help anyone.

When Peter finds himself on a mountaintop confronted with the most glorious, and perhaps most terrifying, sight of his life, he doesn't fare much better than I did on the pool table.

Mountain encounter

The story begins six days after the disastrous exchange in which Jesus called Peter Satan. Jesus invited Peter, James, and John up onto a high mountain. These guys were Jesus' inner circle. Not because Jesus had favourites, but because you can't get anything done if everyone gets an equal turn at everything.

Suddenly, without warning, on top of the mountain, Jesus was transformed. His clothes became dazzling white, and he shone like the sun. Jesus no longer just looked like any old Middle Eastern dude; he looked like a bright, shining, supernaturally radiant Middle Eastern dude. And he was joined by two more Middle Eastern dudes, Elijah and Moses, who were talking to Jesus (Mark 9:2–4).

All this raises a few questions for me. First, how did the disciples know it was Elijah and Moses? Mark doesn't record that Jesus introduced anyone ('Peter, James, and John, I'd like you to meet Elijah and Moses'), and it's not like there were photographs around from which the disciples could recognise them. Were they wearing name tags? Did an angelic MC recite a pithy bio before they appeared? Why has no one explained this?

Second, what were Jesus, Elijah, and Moses talking about? What does anyone talk about when you suddenly appear on a mountaintop next to Jesus? One minute you're in heaven reading a good book, then suddenly you're plonked next to Jesus somewhere in Israel for a quick summit on the summit. Was it a high-minded conversation that you could only understand if you've passed into glory, or was it more mundane stuff? Perhaps Moses remarked, 'So, this is the Promised Land! I never actually got to see it!' and maybe Elijah complained, 'Look at the traffic these days, and all that new development. Things were much nicer here in my day.' Who knows! Whatever they were saying, I like that they were talking with Jesus. Despite the solemness of the occasion, it wasn't too solemn for a little chit-chat.[34]

It was at this point that Peter felt the need to pipe up. There he was, faced with the most awesome moment of his life – meeting two heroes of his faith and his master getting transformed into some fantastic human sun. He had no category of experience into which he could fit this unique event, and he thought to himself, 'This is intense! There are Elijah and Moses, heroes from the Scriptures, talking with our leader! The only thing that could make this moment better would be for me to say something.' So his solution was to say some strange things.

First, he said, 'Rabbi, it is good for us to be here' (Mark 9:5). Why did he think he was of any kind of importance to that moment? He was not a vital player. It's as if Peter thought Elijah and Moses just accidentally appeared on that mountain after an unfortunate mishap with time travelling, and by sheer luck they just happened to have arrived where Peter, James, and John were. What good thing did Peter think he, James, and John could do?

'Let us put up three shelters – one for you, one for Moses and one for Elijah,' Peter says next (v. 5). He seems to have thought the best response was to set up camp

---

34. In Luke's account we *are* told what they were talking about: 'Two men, Moses and Elijah, appeared in glorious splendour, talking with Jesus. They spoke about his departure, which he was about to bring to fulfillment at Jerusalem' (Luke 9:30–31). I didn't include this in the main text because I like the idea of Elijah complaining about traffic, and I suspect that if Elijah and Moses did turn up they would have had time for small talk before getting down to the business of talking about Jesus' impending death, resurrection, and ascension.

for these three guys. Whether they were to be temporary shelters to protect them from the heat of the sun as they talked, or tents so they could have a good old camp out on the top of the mountain, is not clear. Perhaps Peter was envisioning them having long chats into the night around the campfire, toasting marshmallows, singing songs together, and giving their testimonies. I don't know. None of it really seems that logical. Which makes sense, because the next thing that Mark writes is this: '(He did not know what to say, they were so frightened)' (v. 6).

Peter was just talking. He was so scared, he just talked, and he said whatever came to mind, which didn't turn out to be anything useful at all.

All his talk seems even more absurd when you read what happens next: 'Then a cloud appeared and covered them, and a voice came from the cloud: "This is my Son, whom I love. Listen to him!"' (v. 7).

As the cloud appeared and the voice of God spoke, he called on Peter, James, and John to do the exact opposite of what Peter had been doing: listen. Despite all of Peter's talking, it was time for God to speak and Peter to listen. There was nothing for Peter to add – he should have said nothing at all.

The mountain men

Perhaps at this point it might be worth considering why Elijah and Moses were the ones who appeared on the mountain with Jesus. Why not Noah? Why not King David? Why not Jael, who stabbed a guy through the head with a tent peg (Judges 4:17–22)?

You may remember from the stories of Moses and Elijah that both of them had significant encounters with God on mountains. Moses, after leading the people of Israel out of Egypt, arrived at the foot of Mount Sinai. From there, God summoned Moses up the mountain to meet with him. For forty days Moses was in God's presence, receiving the law. At one point, after Moses' first encounter with God on the mountain, and after he smashed the Ten Commandments in anger at the people of Israel, Moses was feeling despondent and asked God to show him his glory. God responded:

> 'I will cause all my goodness to pass in front of you, and I will proclaim my name, the Lord, in your presence. I will have mercy on whom I will have mercy, and I will have compassion on whom I will have compassion. But,' he said, 'you cannot see my face, for no one may see me and live.'
>
> Then the Lord said, 'There is a place near me where you may stand on a rock. When my glory passes by, I will put you in a cleft in the rock and cover you with my hand until I have passed by. Then I will remove my hand and you will see my back; but my face must not be seen.' (Exodus 33:19–23)

So the next day, Moses went back up the mountain and God came by proclaiming his name to Moses:

> 'The Lord, the Lord, the compassionate and gracious God, slow to anger, abounding in love and faithfulness, maintaining love to thousands, and forgiving wickedness, rebellion and sin. Yet he does not leave the guilty unpunished; he punishes the children and their children for the sin of the parents to the third and fourth generation.'
>
> Moses bowed to the ground at once and worshipped. (Exodus 34:6–8)

In Moses' encounter on the mountain, God told him his name, and it's a very long name! (It's also difficult to distinguish between God's first, middle, and last names, but that's beside the point.) Moses had one of the greatest encounters with God in the entire Bible, and still all he could see was God's back. If that is what happens when someone sees God's back, imagine seeing God face to face?

This brings us to Elijah and his encounter with God. You may know the story of Elijah and the prophets of Baal. It's in 1 Kings 18. Israel had been living in the Promised Land for many, many years. The people there had been seduced by other gods and were worshipping them instead of Yahweh, the one true God. (Yahweh is the proper name of God that he proclaimed to Moses. When he said, 'The Lord, the Lord' he was saying 'Yahweh, Yahweh.') So Elijah set up a contest between Yahweh and Baal, the false god of one of the surrounding nations. He challenged the prophets of Baal to call down fire from heaven on one of their sacrifices. Then Elijah would call on God to bring down fire on his sacrifice. As you would expect, Yahweh won the contest handily. The prophets of Baal couldn't even get a spark, but God consumed the entire cow and the altar it had been laid upon. The people all fell on their faces, worshipping God, saying, 'The Lord – he is God! The Lord – he is God!' (1 Kings 18:39).

This should have been one of the great high points of Elijah's life, but after he received a threat against his life from Israel's queen, he fell into a deep depression, and he went out into the wilderness to die. There, God sent an angel to minister to him, who gave him food, drink, and a nap. After this Elijah got up and travelled for forty days to the very same mountain that Moses was on when he met with God. There he settled down in a cave for the night.

In the cave God spoke to him: 'What are you doing here, Elijah?' (1 Kings 19:9).

Elijah replied, 'I have been very zealous for the Lord God Almighty. The Israelites have rejected your covenant, torn down your altars, and put your prophets to death with the sword. I am the only one left, and now they are trying to kill me too' (v. 10).

So God told him to go stand on the mountain 'in the presence of the Lord, for the Lord is about to pass by' (v. 11). Sounds familiar doesn't it? This is what happened next:

Then a great and powerful wind tore the mountains apart and shattered the rocks before the Lord, but the Lord was not in the wind. After the wind there was an earthquake, but the Lord was not in the earthquake. After the earthquake came a fire, but the Lord was not in the fire. And after the fire came a gentle whisper. When Elijah heard it, he pulled his cloak over his face and went out and stood at the mouth of the cave.

Then a voice said to him, 'What are you doing here, Elijah?'

He replied, 'I have been very zealous for the Lord God Almighty. The Israelites have rejected your covenant, torn down your altars, and put your prophets to death with the sword. I am the only one left, and now they are trying to kill me too.' (vv. 11–14)

Elijah did encounter God, but it wasn't in the same way that Moses did. Elijah needed something different. For him, he didn't need the bombast of trumpets, fire, or earthquakes; he'd just seen God's glory on the mountain with the prophets of Baal. Elijah needed to hear God's gentle whisper. He needed to meet God in the silence of his depression.

And notice that their conversation didn't change. God asked the same question, and Elijah gave the same answer. Only then did God send Elijah back to finish the work he had been called to.

Listen

Hopefully now it's clear why Jesus was with Elijah and Moses. Here were two men who met God on a mountain, now with the God-man on a mountain. Whatever encounter they had had with God, this was greater. This was God in the flesh, face to face, not speaking only once but always speaking as the Word of God incarnate. When Moses and Elijah disappeared, leaving only Jesus, those two great men of the Old Covenant gave way to the ultimate greatness of Jesus. The God of the mountain was now there, on earth, dwelling among humanity. How should one respond? God spoke, affirming Jesus and spelling out the correct response: listen. Peter, James, and John were to listen to Jesus. The disciples were to listen to Jesus. All of us who meet Jesus are to listen to him.

What did Jesus do then? Did he give a speech? Did he whisper a prophecy? No. The wondrous event ended, and they walked down off the mountain: 'Suddenly, when they looked around, they no longer saw anyone with them except Jesus. As they were coming down the mountain, Jesus gave them orders not to tell anyone what they had seen until the Son of Man had risen from the dead' (Mark 9:8–9).

God's command to the three disciples was not a set of instructions, but a way to be. To be listeners. It would be easy to listen to Jesus on the mountain, amid the glorious conference of Bible heroes, but what about when they were off the mountain, and there were no bright transfigurations? No Old Testament heroes? No voices from heaven? Would they listen to him there? They were no less meeting with God as they walked the paths of Israel, avoiding animal dung and feeling the pain in their heels as their tempers frayed and they wondered when they might get to rest for the day. Even then, they were in the midst of God's presence. Would they listen to Jesus in normal life? Would Peter be able to tell when his suggestions were just as silly as building tents for dead heroes, even when the context seemed less solemn?

I don't think Jesus meant the most important lessons for Peter, James, and John to be learnt while they were up on the mountain, but when they came down. They had to remember that Jesus was still worth listening to and following when he annoyed them, when he asked them to do tough things, when their enemies were arrayed against them, and when it looked like those enemies had defeated him. It was always important to remember to listen to him as God's Son.

The instruction that Jesus gave them, not to tell anyone about what had happened until he had risen from the dead, meant that Jesus wanted the moment to be understood in light of his death and resurrection. If they just worshipped Jesus as the exalted Son of God, greater than Moses and Elijah, without also remembering his death on a cross and his resurrection, they would continue to make the same mistake that we read about Peter making in the last chapter – assuming that Jesus didn't need to go to the cross. But when we view Jesus' greatest glory as coming not on that mountain with Moses and Elijah but on the lonely hill outside Jerusalem as he died a criminal's death, then we can properly understand and listen to Jesus.

What does it mean to listen to Jesus as the glorious Son of God who died and rose again? It means we don't have to be afraid that if we were to meet with God he would destroy us. Jesus took care of that. It means we don't have to make up suggestions for what might be useful. It means we listen to his commands and follow him wherever he leads. Even if he takes us down off the mountain, into the darkest valleys, we know he is as much God in the magnificent moments as in the most evil events. We can trust him, even if he leads us into death, because we've seen our future on the other side in the glorified, resurrected Jesus.

If you're a follower of Jesus, you too have encountered God. You have had the greatest encounter with God. Perhaps there was not fire, smoke, clouds, loud voices, or glowing clothes, but the testimony of the Bible is that the Spirit of Christ lives within you (1 Corinthians 3:16). This might feel a bit ho-hum, but think about what that means: everywhere you go, everything you do, you have Jesus with you by his Holy Spirit.

Do you identify with the 'mountaintop experience'? The feeling you get after being at an amazing Christian camp, or in a powerful church service, when you've sung great songs and heard from the Bible and had excellent times of prayer and encouragement from Christian friends and you feel you've just met with

God. You come away from those times feeling like you will spend your whole life serving Jesus.

But as you come down off the mountain, the daily grind of life gets in the way. You get up early for school or work, deal with due dates and deadlines, and just generally get distracted by games, Netflix, or your favourite book. Will you still remember that you can meet with God – that you can hear from Jesus?

And when you're in the most painful moments of your life – when you're sick, when a loved one has died, when you're battling mental illness, when you've committed a most terrible sin, or when your doubts seem to be overwhelming you – will you remember that the Jesus you met on the mountain is the same one who will meet you in the depths of pain? The same one who knows the way to the other side? The one who will give you the power to emerge alive on the other side of death?

Will you listen to him?

You might be thinking, 'Okay, yes, but *how* do I listen to him? I don't get to meet Jesus face to face like the disciples did.' It's true, you don't. But to some degree you have more than the disciples did. You have the stories that the disciples passed on about Jesus. You have the stories and letters of the early church as they figured out what Jesus was calling them to. You have the histories, poetry, and prophecies of God's people from before Jesus, that now, in the light of Jesus, show off their deepest truths. All of this is in the Bible. And all of this gives us insights into Jesus that the disciples didn't have while he was on earth. The Bible is the primary place where we can listen to Jesus.

That said, it's not just a matter of reading the Bible for ten minutes a day and saying, 'There! I've heard from Jesus' and getting on with your life as if nothing has changed. No, you must ask Jesus to speak to you through the Bible, then as you read, you ask Jesus what he's saying to you. As you go through your day, you reflect and see how what you read might be Jesus speaking to the situation you are in. The more you get to know Jesus through the Bible, the better you will hear what he is saying to you in your life.

When the Holy Spirit prompts you – through your thoughts, through a friend encouraging or challenging you, through someone's preaching, in the lyrics of a song, or even through nature – you'll know how to recognise his voice, because what he says will be the same voice you hear in the Bible. When you have a feeling that God is speaking to you, but you're unsure if it's just your thoughts, your emotions, or God himself, you'll know how to recognise his voice, because you've heard it first in Scripture.

I know Bible reading and reflection doesn't seem exciting or novel, but there is a reason why people have been doing it for thousands of years. It's because it works. It's because Jesus has never stopped speaking, and he'll speak to you now, in your most exciting times and your hardest moments.

The disciples got to spend every day encountering God himself in Jesus. This was not just during a glorious mountain experience, but in their everyday, mundane life. They heard Jesus speaking; they only needed to listen. Because Jesus lives with you by his Spirit, you too can hear him speaking, if only you would listen. Will you?

8

'BURN THEM ALL'

The Disciples Want to Call Down Fire on Samaritans
Luke 9:51–56

I love guns, tanks, and fighter jets. Also, I'm a pacifist. Once when I was on holidays with my friends, I was walking around the streets of Adelaide, and we passed an indoor shooting range. Being Australian city boys, we never had much of a chance to shoot guns, but it seemed like this place just let anyone walk in off the street and destroy a few paper targets. That was our kind of holiday fun. We handed over our hard-earned dollarydoos and were ushered into a concrete bunker to choose our weapons. They showed us Desert Eagles, Colt .45s, and my favourite, the Glock 9mm. I liked the Glock because I had seen it in movies a lot, and I love movies. I chose to shoot the Glock. Boy, was it fun. Loud, powerful, and dangerous.

I was a terrible shot. Fifty per cent of the time I didn't even hit the target. I didn't really care though. I was just having fun. Because I love guns.

Did I mention I also love tanks? And fighter jets? Every now and again I go watch an air show, and the best bit is when the fighter jets come screaming through the sky. They are so loud you feel it in your chest. They'll do a low pass, and sometimes there will even be pyrotechnics, with fireballs exploding across the airfield as if they've just done a bombing run. So much noise! So much fire!

But, despite this love of violent technology, I hate violence. I hate what guns, tanks, and fighter jets are used for. Sure, I know sometimes they are a deterrent to stop other people using guns, tanks, and planes, but really I wish they only existed for shooting ranges, air shows, and movies. I'm aware that war is a much more profitable business than entertaining plane nerds and forcefully subduing paper targets, but we can dream of a world where things only get blown up for entertainment and nobody gets hurt, can't we?

While there weren't any fighter jets or guns available in the days of the disciples, the desire to see things blow up seems to be a rather universal trait that crosses the barriers of time and culture.

Sky fire

Luke begins the story by telling us that Jesus and his disciples 'resolutely set out for Jerusalem' (Luke 9:51). This wasn't because Jesus just really liked Jerusalem – like say when I'm determined to get home because

I like my couch and I have a lot of Netflix to watch.
Jerusalem was where everything would go down. It was
where Jesus would be put to trial, executed, rise again,
and then ascend into heaven. This was about heading to
the climax of Jesus' story. It was the beginning of Jesus'
journey to complete his mission. If the book of Luke was
a movie, this would be the beginning of a travel montage
as Jesus and his crew went from town to town, preparing
for the big showdown with the Pharisees.

We're told that as Jesus travelled, he sent messengers
ahead of him to get things ready (v. 52). Whether they
were looking for places for Jesus to stay or to preach,
the Bible isn't clear. Some of these messengers went to
a Samaritan village. Samaritans and Jews didn't really
get on very well. Each group thought the other had
perverted the true religion, and they saw them as dirty
heretics. This is why the parable of the good Samaritan
(coming up in the very next chapter of Luke) was so
confronting. To imagine a Samaritan acting with more
love and mercy than Jewish holy men was ludicrous to
the Jewish listeners.

Jesus, on the other hand, was not an intolerant
guy. He was happy to associate with anyone and invite
everyone into relationship with God. So hanging out
with a bunch of Samaritans wouldn't bother him at all
(see John 4). Unfortunately, the Samaritans weren't as
open to having Jesus visit, and they refused to welcome
him (Luke 9:53).

Now Jesus had prepared for just such an eventuality.
He knew that he and his disciples weren't always going

to be welcome, so he gave this teaching to his disciples as he sent them out to preach, teach, and heal, which we read at the beginning of chapter nine: 'Whatever house you enter, stay there until you leave that town. If people do not welcome you, leave their town and shake the dust off your feet as a testimony against them' (Luke 9:4–5).

This may seem like odd behaviour: 'Was someone mean to you? Clean your feet.' But it's the ancient equivalent of brushing your shoulder off. Although, as you brush off your feet, you're not just saying, 'This is not my concern,' you're also saying, 'These people are God's concern, he can deal with them.' Brushing your feet off is about the least violent form of protest you can get. Nobody even does any shouting!

So what happens when Jesus is rejected by the Samaritans? Do the disciples remember his teaching for just this eventuality? Nope! James and John (whom Jesus fittingly called the 'sons of thunder', remember?) turn to Jesus and ask, 'Lord, do you want us to call fire down from heaven to destroy them?' (v. 54).

It's quite an escalation from 'Let's brush our feet off' to 'LET'S BLOW THEM UP WITH SKY FIRE!' Why they think they have the ability to call heaven's napalm, I'm not sure. Perhaps they reckon they can get Jesus' power by proxy. I imagine that hanging out with Jesus can make one feel rather powerful. I feel powerful when I hang out with people who know martial arts, so being around Jesus must be intoxicating.

James and John seem to have remembered a story about Elijah where he calls down fire on a bunch of

Samaritan soldiers (2 Kings 1). Growing up hearing those stories as small Israelite boys, the Thunder Sons probably thought Elijah was awesome. And now, after their encounter with Jesus, Moses, and Elijah on the mountaintop, they probably realised that, as they were with someone greater than Elijah, they might get to see some fireworks greater than Elijah's! It totally makes sense.

Imagine if Jesus had said 'Sure thing!' and then James and John prayed, and fifty Samaritans were blown from the face of the earth? That would be a very different Jesus to the one we're used to. Just thinking about that makes me feel a little queasy (although movies about Jesus would have way more explosions, which is a definite plus).

What did Jesus do instead? He rebuked them (v. 55). Why? Because Jimmy and Johnny hadn't really understood Jesus. They understood his power, but they hadn't understood his mission. They looked at the Samaritans, saw them as enemies, and longed for their destruction. They didn't understand that while judgement was coming, they didn't get to decide who deserved it and who didn't. And they definitely didn't understand that before judgement would fall on anyone else, it would fall on Jesus. Jesus came not to destroy people, but to receive our destruction upon himself, so that anyone might find forgiveness and be welcomed into the family of God.

Your Samaritans

There's a challenge in this story of intolerance and enemy-hating for us, too. Chances are we're not hoping to rain fire from the sky on the people in the next suburb or the shop assistant who was rude to us, but I doubt we're too far removed from James and John's desire for destruction of people we don't like.

I used to work as a gas meter reader. This meant that I would walk the streets and read the numbers on people's gas meters so the gas company could send them a bill. As you can imagine, people were always thrilled to see me coming. They would welcome me with lemonade and cookies. Everyone loves getting bills.

For most houses the gas meter was in the front yard, so one thing I was trained to do was to keep an eye out for dogs. The machines we used to record the gas readings would also give us a warning if there was known to be a dog on the property. Most dogs are pretty friendly, but some dogs are not. Or at least not to the random human who just rocks up in their territory uninvited.

When I first started the job, I wasn't too worried about dogs, because most of my life I have had pretty good interactions with dogs. But then I'd walk up to gates and fences trying to figure out if it was safe to enter the yard, and dogs would come bounding out of nowhere yelling, 'Get away! If you take one step into my yard, I'll rip your throat out with my teeth!' Well, that's what I assume they were saying. None of the dogs I met spoke English. For the small dogs, I found this was amusing, for the big dogs, it was terrifying. Usually when this happened, I just left the house alone. Those people just didn't get their gas meter read. I'm sure they were very disappointed.

Every now and again, I'd go into a yard, where there was no sign of a dog, and my machine hadn't told me about a dog, when suddenly, out of nowhere, there was a dog yelling, 'GET OUT OF MY YARD! I'LL KILL YOU! I'LL KILL YOU!' to which I'd respond, 'I'm leaving, I'm leaving!' The dog may not have spoken English to me, but I spoke English to the dog, just in case it was bilingual.

After a few encounters with angry dogs, I started to get stressed by any dog. Unless they were overtly friendly (and I met a few of those), I would assume every dog was a threat. I would see a dog in a yard, happily sleeping in the sun, and I'd think, 'You're probably out to kill me.' Even when I met dogs and I wasn't working, I would feel threatened by them. There were probably a lot of kind dogs who I didn't get to pet because a few angry dogs ruined it for me. A few mean dogs made every dog a threat.

You may see where I'm going with this. Sometimes, we can approach people in a similar way. We may have had a nasty experience with a person from a particular social or cultural group, and so we now feel threatened by everyone who fits that type. Or we have been told by our parents, or our friends, society, religious leaders, or social media that a certain kind of person is evil, or out to get us and destroy our way of life. Those people then become a threat to us, so we feel a mix of anger, fear, and hatred, or merely disinterest towards them. We can classify people as a threat because of their race, religion, class, sexuality, political views, gender, or more. When we view groups of people as a threat, we are on the same path as James and John.

Who are the people who threaten you? Who are the people you wish God's punishment upon? Or who are the people who you really just wish terrible things would happen to, either by your hands or the hands of others? Is it people of a different faith to you? Is it people who seem to be dragging their heels on addressing climate change? Is it the immigrants who are moving into your suburb and bringing their culture with them? Is it the people who believe and say different things to you about gender and sexuality? Is it the people who have different expressions of their gender or sexuality to you? Who are you threatened by? Who are your Samaritans?

When we realise whom we're threatened by, we have to decide what we will do about them. Hopefully, it's obvious that the option of fire from heaven is off the table. But what should we do? The first thing is actually really easy: do nothing. Notice in Luke 9 that Jesus didn't really do anything about the Samaritans. He didn't attack them, he didn't speak badly about them, and he didn't complain about them. He and the disciples just went to a different village (v. 56). He brushed the rejection off.

Sometimes the best thing to do is nothing. Did someone upset you? Don't overreact and call down verbal fire upon them, don't complain to all your friends, don't rant on the socials. Brush it off. Is there a group of people who really get you going? Don't do anything. Leave them alone. Do a Jesus, do nothing.

'Ahh. Do nothing. I can do that.' Yes, you can. It's probably some of the simplest advice ever given. Brush your feet off, leave God to deal with them. But that's not really the end of the story. Because while Jesus was done with the Samaritans then, he wasn't done with them for good.

Later in this book we will talk about what happened after Jesus' resurrection, but I'll give you a bit of a preview now. In Acts 1, after he had died and risen and was about to head off into heaven to rule the universe from there, Jesus gave his apostles a job to do. He wanted them to go into the world and be witnesses to the fact that he died and rose again. So he sent them to Jerusalem (where they were, their holy city), to Judea (the area surrounding Jerusalem), to Samaria (the land of their enemies with the hybrid religion), to the ends of the earth (everywhere beyond Samaria, like Rome, Shanghai, Nebaj, and Hobart) (Acts 1:8).[35] Jesus didn't want to blow up the Samaritans, and he wasn't neutral about them. He wanted them to come to faith in him, and he sent the same men who wanted to see them

---

35. In case you're wondering, Nebaj is a town in Guatemala that I found on Google maps. It is home to an eating establishment called 'Restaurante Lemon Light' which has 3.8 stars on Google, so if you ever visit, you could think about eating there. Hobart is the capital city of Tasmania, an island state off the south coast of Australia, which is famous for having some markets and an art gallery with a machine that makes poop. For an adventure I had in Hobart, see Chapter 12.

vapourised by angels with flamethrowers, to be the ones to invite them to be part of the people of God.

What this means for us is that Jesus doesn't want us to only brush our enemies off, but to actively seek their good. He wants us to go to them, to build relationships with them, to bless them, and to invite them into God's family.

It might take you a little while to move from wanting to destroy a person to wanting to see them flourish and saved. It wasn't an immediate change in the disciples, and Jesus might have to do some work in you, too. You might have to spend a bit of time in the first stage, doing nothing, leaving them alone, and praying that God might help you to trust him to deal with them. But soon, you should begin to pray for them, not just about them. You should pray that God might bless them as Jesus commanded (Luke 6:27–28). As you do this, you should work towards actively doing good things for them. This might even be through finding a way to build relationships with them.

Sven from Sweden

At my high school, there were a group of guys whose parents had migrated to Australia, and they would all hang out together and harass anyone who got in their way. I'm not going to tell you which country they had emigrated from because that doesn't really matter and I don't want to fuel any racism, but for the sake of the story, we'll say they were from Sweden. (They weren't Swedish, so please don't let this story fuel any Ikea hate you might be harbouring.) There were plenty of friendly Swedes at my school, but as they weren't mean I tended not to notice them. I did notice the group who would hang out together and walk around like they owned the school. Almost all them were younger than me so didn't bother me much, but I still found them rather intimidating. There was one guy who took a particular dislike to me and my friends. We'll call him Sven. Sven would say rude stuff to us and get in our way. One of my friends liked to talk back, so Sven would make sure to push him around and threaten him whenever he saw us. The Swedes in general, and Sven in particular, made me wary of any Nordic people I encountered in my life. I didn't want to be racist, but I could feel the growing resentment inside me.

One day at school, I was making a video project for drama, and I had written a part for a bully. Seeing as Sven was the most bully-like bully I knew, I thought, 'I should get Sven to be the bully.' This seemed like both a terrible idea and a great one. I knew he'd do an outstanding job, and I also had an inkling that getting him onboard might improve our relationship. We had a mutual friend, so I asked her to introduce us. She made the introduction, I nervously asked him to be in the film, and he was incredulous that I would want him.

'You want me to be in your film? Really? But I can't act. I can't do it. I can't do it.'

When he wasn't being a bully, he was behaving like pretty much anyone else who doesn't act when you ask them to act – nervous. But I convinced him, and he agreed to come to the shoot. (The fact that our drama teacher would get him out of class to do it may also have helped.)

When the shoot day came, these words of Jesus' weighed on my mind: 'Love your enemies, do good to those who hate you, bless those who curse you, pray for those who ill-treat you' (Luke 6:27–28). The Holy Spirit wanted me to know that I had a job to do. I was nervous when Sven turned up. My friends who were helping as the crew and the other actors were there. I hoped he would not be rude or beat us up, but he turned out to be the most timid of anyone in the room. We had food and drink for the actors – barbecue chicken, hot chips, and Coke. We were very professional. I showed Sven the spread and told him he could have any of it. He didn't understand.

'I can eat any of this?'

'Yes.' I replied. 'You're helping make the film. It's for you.'

He couldn't quite believe it. When the time came to shoot his scene, he did exactly what I wanted him to do. He was the perfect bully. The only problem with Sven was that when he had to push the main character (something I'd seen him do to others many times) he was too gentle. He didn't want to hurt anyone. But we got there in the end. Sven did an expert job, and I thanked him profusely for his contribution to the movie.

Did I ever get to tell him the gospel? I wish I could say I did, and that Sven is now a pastor of a church or something, but that's not true. But I'll tell you what did

142

happen: my relationship with Sven got a lot better. We would say 'Hi' to each other in the halls, which was a long way from trying to avoid him in case he threatened me or my friends. And the whole thing made me feel a lot better about people from Sweden. I was reminded that they were all just people who, like everyone, get nervous about acting. And just like the rest of us, Sven's meanness, gentleness, nervousness, and kindness came not from his belonging to any particular group of people, but to the fact that he was as complex and enmeshed in his world as I am in mine.

I am pretty good at the 'brush the dust off your feet' part of Jesus' teaching. I dislike confrontation, so just leaving people alone works well for me. But actively doing good things for them is a lot harder for me. Sven the Swede helped teach me that kindness is better than avoidance. If I'm willing to risk love, I might see some surprising results.

Who are the Samaritans in your life? Who, like James and John, might you want to see destroyed? Where is Jesus calling you to leave someone alone – to lay aside your desire for vengeance? And whose good could Jesus be asking you to seek? Could he even be asking you to share the most ultimate good with them, the good news of Jesus? Jesus turned us, his enemies, into friends. He didn't seek our destruction but our salvation. When we join the mission of Jesus, we join his mission of helping all people to know God's goodness, no matter who they are. We can leave judgement to God. Our job is to seek goodness and salvation for all.

9

LET THE LITTLE CHILDREN GET LOST

Jesus and the Children
Mark 10:13–16

Picture this scene. Jesus is in a house with his disciples. One of the disciples asks him a question, so Jesus stops and begins to answer the question, taking the opportunity to give some teaching. People know that Jesus is in the front room of this house, so they poke their heads in to hear what he has to say. As he speaks, crowds are gathering, spilling out the door, straining to hear. People are craning their necks to look through the window. As they listen, they realise this is something they have never heard before. His message is world changing. They are mesmerised. And then someone interjects.

'Excuse me, Jesus?' They push through the crowd to get to Jesus, holding something small in their arms. 'Um... I don't mean to interrupt but I'm wondering if you might be willing to give a quick blessing to my guinea pig. I want her to have a really good life.'

'Oh yeah, Jesus!' yells another, as they barge past the other blessing seekers. 'Please bless my rat.'

'Jesus! I've brought my pet snake!'

Within moments there are animal lovers everywhere, coming at Jesus with all manner of strange pets, hoping that he might give them a blessing. The disciples realise what's happening. Dealing with all these people's kooky animal requests is going to derail Jesus from his real ministry. So they start sending the petting zoo and their owners away.

'Jesus doesn't have time to be blessing pets. Let someone else do that!'

As they try to manage the menagerie, Jesus has an inscrutable look on his face. What does he think about all this?

How do you feel about the actions of the disciples? Do you agree with them? Do you think that Jesus shouldn't be sidetracked by an inconsequential ministry? Or do you think he really should be spending his time blessing people's weird pets? Is your picture of Jesus that he is so kind and loving he's even got time for a pet tarantula named Gary?

This story is not in the Bible, but there is one a bit like it. People didn't bring iguanas and ferrets to Jesus for a blessing; they brought kids. And the disciples were having none of it.

Not pets, but people

In Mark 10 we read that, after a time of teaching about divorce, 'People were bringing little children to Jesus for him to place his hands on them' (v. 13). One of the things that people liked to do in Jesus' day was to get the rabbis, the spiritual teachers, to bless their kids before their first birthday. Perhaps this was like a spiritual version of getting your kid's photo taken with Santa.

While these days we think kids are pretty special, and we definitely love babies, in ancient Israelite society people didn't like them nearly as much. For us, kids often become the centre of family life. Parents spend a lot of energy organising their life around their kids, making sure they get good schooling and attending all their extra-curricular activities. Weekends become about getting the kids from one thing to another. When choosing where to go on holidays, families are always looking for something child friendly. Children are pretty darn important. If you're a kid yourself, you're probably not too upset by this situation.

In Jesus' society, kids were often loved by their parents, and were seen as a blessing from God, but everything didn't revolve around them. Kids had a job to do. That was to grow up, help in the family business, learn a trade, and look after their parents. The boys had to reproduce and continue the family name.

147

In Roman society, kids were there to serve the needs of the parents. It's shocking to think about, but if the parents weren't happy with their babies, they could abandon them by leaving them in a town square or on a rubbish dump, and there would be no consequences. This often happened to children who were female or had a disability.

So when people started bringing their kids to Jesus for a blessing, the disciples weren't thinking, 'How adorable, we need to get a good shot of Jesus kissing a baby,' as if he were some politician looking to get elected. They saw women (people of low importance), with babies (people of least importance), interrupting the teacher (the person of most importance). The disciples were having none of it! So they 'rebuked them' (v. 13). You can imagine it, can't you?

'What do you think you're doing, lady?' the disciples may have said. 'The teacher doesn't have time for your crying baby. No one can hear him over your kid's screaming!' The women would have loved their kids, but the disciples just saw them as an annoying and unnecessary distraction.

The problem is, just one chapter earlier in Mark, Jesus had something to say about kids – and it wasn't that they should be sent away till they're contributing members of society.

Jesus and the disciples were on the road together, and Jesus predicted his death. You can be sure that whenever Jesus predicts his death, the disciples do something daft, and this time was no different. As they travelled along, they didn't discuss what it meant that Jesus was going to die; they argued over who was the greatest. When they arrived at Capernaum, Jesus asked them, 'What were you arguing about on the road?' (Mark 9:33). But no one said anything, because they were understandably embarrassed that they'd been caught having a selfish argument. Verses 35–37 say: 'Sitting down, Jesus called the Twelve and said, "Anyone who wants to be first must be the very last, and the servant of all." He took a little child whom he placed among them. Taking the child in his arms, he said to them, "Whoever welcomes one of these little children in my name welcomes me; and whoever welcomes me does not welcome me but the one who sent me."'

Jesus was making a clear statement about what it means to be great. In God's upside-down kingdom, greatness comes from humility, and being first means putting others before yourself. Jesus illustrated this by inviting a child into his group. He was teaching them that how you treat the weakest of people, like children, has a direct connection to how you treat him, and how you treat him indicates how you treat God himself. So rather than seeking to align yourself with the most powerful, Jesus was saying, 'When you make room for the least powerful, you make room for me.'

I'm sure all the disciples heard this, nodded, and went away thinking about how they needed to be more polite to kids.

But only a few days later, they had entirely forgotten Jesus' teaching. Here were some parents with their children, and the disciples weren't welcoming them; they were rebuking them. They thought they were doing the work of Jesus, but according to Jesus' teaching, they were actually rejecting him!

If you've ever made a decision to commit yourself to some new way of obeying Jesus, and then quickly gone and done the opposite, take heart that the disciples did exactly the same thing.

So Jesus saw what was going on, and funnily enough, he wasn't happy. He was about to do the thing that Mum and Dad do when they catch you doing something you have just been warned about: 'WHAT DID I JUST TELL YOU?'

Jesus didn't quite say that, but Mark does write that he was 'indignant', which I'm happy to assume means that he said something of the sort. What he said was this: 'Let the little children come to me, and do not hinder them, for the kingdom of God belongs to such as these. Truly I tell you, anyone who will not receive the kingdom of God like a little child will never enter it' (Mark 10:14–15).

Jesus was saying that the kingdom of God is not for the powerful or the influential. Instead, it belongs to those who will enter it not on their own merits but on their own dependence. Kids are dependent and, in Jesus' day, totally lacking in power. We may think that God would want us in his kingdom because of what we can contribute, but our entrance relies on us realising that all we can contribute is our helpless faith in Jesus to welcome us in.

The disciples definitely hadn't figured this out. First they wanted to blow up the Samaritans, and now this – they clearly had to learn lessons at least twice. Jesus had just said that if you welcome the kids, you welcome him, so this was their chance to do just that, but here they were rebuking the people who were bringing their kids to Jesus. So Jesus instead took the children into his arms and blessed them. As he welcomed them to himself, he lived out the words that he had so recently spoken. The children were being received by the King of the kingdom.

You and the powerless

The disciples were not powerful people in their society; they were young men who had little money and influence following a controversial teacher around the countryside. So it's no wonder that when they got the chance to exercise some power, they took it. As they rebuked the parents with their kids, perhaps they were on a bit of a power trip, enjoying the opportunity to be bouncers for Jesus.[36]

I remember when I first started high school, I hated being one of the smallest people in the school. We little Year 7s would get pushed around by pretty much everyone else. We always got the worst seats in assembly, on the bus, and on the train. I was an extra small Year 7 kid, so I got pushed around even by the kids in my year.

36. Incidentally, if this book writing thing doesn't work out, I'll probably start my own nightclub security business and call it Bouncers for Jesus.

I remember once holding the door to the library open for a load of kids, and the bully of our year punched me in the stomach as he walked past. For what reason, I'm unsure. Maybe I was holding the door wrong.

What all this meant was that when I got to Year 8, I was pretty excited not to be the smallest in the school. There was a new batch of Year 7s coming, and I could push them around. On the first day of school, as we were all getting off the bus, I deliberately ran into one of the Year 7s. I wanted to assert my dominance. I thought it'd feel pretty good, but I just felt unpleasant. Making someone else feel small didn't really make me feel powerful.

On the other hand, in a completely different situation, I once had the keys to the switch to turn on the lights for a local sporting field. Turning them on and off made me feel very powerful, and I didn't have to push any Year 7s around for the privilege.

The way Jesus responds to those without power never belittles them or serves to prop up his power. Of course, Jesus, being God, had all the power in the world. But he never used his power at the expense of others, and he never needed to dominate others to show how powerful he was.

How much power do you feel like you have? My guess is you don't feel all that powerful. But all of us have power, to some degree. And there is a temptation, like the disciples faced, to misuse that power for our own sense of self-worth. On the other hand, we can, like Jesus, use our power for the sake of others, to show them how worthy of love they are. How would it have felt to have been the kid who was welcomed into his circle and to hear that the kingdom of God belongs to people like you? Probably, pretty darn good.

The question is, then, how can you use your power not to go on a power-trip but to love and bless those who are weaker than you?

In John 13 we see the clearest picture of how Jesus uses his power. The event takes place at the Last Supper, just before Jesus is arrested and killed (which we'll cover in Chapter 12), when Jesus meets with the disciples to have a final meal with them. John tells us that Jesus 'knew that the Father had put all things under his power' (John 13:3). So what does he do? He takes off his outer clothes and washes the disciples' feet. This was a role for only the lowest of servants, and yet Jesus was doing it for his disciples. He was doing it as a symbol of what he was about to do when he goes to the cross. There he will die so that the disciples, and all who trust in him, might be washed clean from sin.

Warning: I'm about to talk about domestic abuse. If this is difficult for you, feel free to skip to the next section, or to the end of this chapter, where you can find some resources to help you.

As I have been writing this chapter, I have also been working on a resource for young people about domestic abuse. One of the things I have learned is that domestic abuse is not really about anger that goes too far, or about people not loving those they abuse. Instead, it's about power and control. At the root of domestic abuse are people wanting to dominate and rule those with whom they are in close relationship. Most often this abuse happens from men towards women.[37]

You might think that this isn't something that you'd ever do, and it may never be a problem that you have to deal with. But research says that in Australia, about one in six women and about one in sixteen men have experienced intimate partner violence.[38] This means that, if these trends continue, some of you reading this will become abusers, some of you reading this will be abused, and all of you reading this will know people who are in abusive relationships. I'm not writing this to scare you, only to make you aware that this is a serious problem, and it is even a problem for Christians.

If you're a guy, then we need to be especially attentive to the way that Jesus calls us to use our power. It is never

37. I know that abuse does happen from women towards men, and even kids towards parents. Any instance of abuse is terrible. But looking at the statistics, it's women who are overwhelmingly the most likely victims of domestic abuse. For instance, in Australia, depending on what state they're in, women are three to six times more likely to experience assault from an intimate partner than men. This is a problem that we men have to deal with. https://www.abs.gov.au/ausstats/abs@.nsf/Lookup/by%20Subject/4510.0~2017~Main%20Features~Victims%20of%20Family%20and%20Domestic%20Violence%20Related%20Offences~6

38. Australian Institute of Health and Welfare 2019. *Family, domestic and sexual violence in Australia: continuing the national story 2019*. Cat. no. FDV 3. Canberra: AIHW. 8 https://www.aihw.gov.au/getmedia/b0037b2d-a651-4abf-9f7b-00a85e3de528/aihw-fdv3-FDSV-in-Australia-2019.pdf

right to control or abuse others. We are called to honour and serve those we are in relationship with. Greatness doesn't come from asserting power but from giving it away. Just as God allows us to choose freely how we will relate to him, we must never manipulate people to relate to us in the way we want or force them to do things they do not want to do. The Christian who truly loves does not exercise power and control over others, but serves them and respects their freedom.

Whoever you are, you have a choice about how you will use your power. The question is: how will you use the power you have – in your relationships, in the words you use, in the physical actions you take, and the choices you make – to serve others the way Jesus has served you? How will you care for even the most powerless with the power and influence you have?

You, the powerless

You might be thinking, 'I know I have power, but most of my life I'm in situations where I'm pretty powerless.' There is a significant chance that far from feeling like a powerful person, you identify much more with the kids in this story whom the disciples tried to turn away. You feel ignored and insignificant to the wider world. There are all sorts of people who feel disempowered in our society, and young people are often in this group.

In some ways there are many privileges for young people these days – schooling, social media, sport, and other programs. But despite all that, it's still hard being young. You can feel like all your decisions are made for you, and like you're being left out of the loop on important stuff. You may feel like the people around you have decided who you are based solely on your age, without putting in the effort to get to know you. They think you're lazy and entitled, or that you're ignorant and opinionated, or whatever other stereotypes of young people they have.

The good news of this story is that if you're powerless, you're the very type of person that Jesus is talking about. He's saying that the kingdom of heaven belongs to those who know how powerless they are.

We don't get welcomed into God's kingdom because we have lots of power, a great reputation, or because we've got a heap of influence. God isn't interested in our wealth or our mental capacity. When Jesus says, 'Truly I tell you, anyone who will not receive the kingdom of God like a little child will never enter it,' I don't think he's saying there is anything inherently better about kids. Only that the littlest kid has the least amount of power and is the most reliant on others. The way you can receive the kingdom of God is by relying solely on God's power and trusting that only he can give you want you need.

I quite like eating hot chips. They are one of my favourite foods. Sometimes I'll be out with someone at a cafe, and they'll have ordered some hot chips, and I'll have just ordered a drink, and they'll say, 'Take as many as you want.' And I'll say, 'Thanks', and then take one out of politeness. Then maybe five minutes later I'll take two more. Then five minutes after that I'll take my final two, and they'll have all the rest. Which is weird because I love hot chips, and they offered me hot chips, and they said I could have as many as I want. If I had as many as I wanted, I'd eat all the chips. But instead, I'm thinking to myself, 'How many chips should I take? I didn't order them so I shouldn't eat any, but I don't want to seem rude. If I take three, I'll look greedy. If I take one, I'll look like I'm just being polite. I should take two. Two is the correct amount.' Which is why in the end I've only eaten five because I don't want to look greedy and I don't want to look impolite.

Now offer those same chips to a five-year-old, and they'll destroy them. I remember being that age, and if you had offered the chips to me, I would have eaten, and eaten, and eaten until they were all gone, and then I would have tried to subtly suggest that you could go buy more.

That's the difference between how a kid receives and how a self-conscious adult does. We think we need to earn things, and if we let people know what we want or need, we'll look too vulnerable. But what God offers, we cannot get for ourselves. He is the great hot chips provider. We bring nothing to the table. We need his love, life, grace, and mercy. The quicker we learn that we cannot earn it, but we get to freely receive it, the quicker we can receive the benefits of God's kingdom.

The disciples got a power trip from sending people away from Jesus. If you're feeling powerless, then you have an advantage (even though I'm sure it doesn't feel like it). You aren't trying to pretend you have power;

you know you cannot get what you need. Like the children in the story, you know what it's like to have to rely on others. If you can hold on to your reliance on God, even as you gain more independence and power, you can receive the kingdom of God like a little child.

> *If you are experiencing abuse in any relationship, you are witnessing abuse, or you think you may be being abusive, you can get help. In Australia you can call 1800 RESPECT (1800 737 732), or you can go to the website 1800respect.org.au and use their online chat. If you're not in Australia, google 'Domestic Violence Help' and your country or state name and you should find resources. If you are in immediate danger, call 000 in Australia or whatever the number is for emergency services in your country.*

10

JUDAS THE SCARIOT

Judas Decides to Betray Jesus
John 12:1–10

Who do you think is the best villain you've seen in a movie, or read in a book or comic? Is it one of the Jokers? Or Thanos? Ursula, Scar, or Lord Farquad? Or someone who has turned up in popular culture since I've written this book?[39] We love a juicy baddie. It's the antagonists who make stories interesting.

The Bible has a few bad guys. Obviously, Satan is the big one. There are a bunch of kings in the Old Testament who did terrible things, like murder their siblings or sacrifice their kids to false gods. King Herod, who

---

39. I'm always concerned that my cultural references will date. Like, ten years ago the hottest social media was Facebook. As I write this, Instagram and TikTok are pretty big, but who knows what it will be in ten years' time. Perhaps villains come and go in popularity like apps.

murdered a bunch of babies in an attempt to kill Jesus, is also clearly evil. And then we come to Judas Iscariot, perhaps the most famous of human Bible bad guys. So now that we're coming to the final days of Jesus' life on earth, it might be good if we discuss Judas.

The first thing we should clear up is his name. He was called Judas Iscariot because he came from the city of Kariot.[40] As a kid, I used to think his name was 'Judas the Scariot'. I was sure that scariot was some kind of designation for a betrayer. Like if a disciple, who was a bit of a prankster, might have been called 'Tobias the Scallywag', Judas, because he was a betrayer, was a scariot. Sometimes I even thought, 'Why did Jesus let him be a disciple? He was clearly evil, everyone called him a scariot for goodness sake!' But in case you're making the same mistake as me, his name is about where he's from, not who he is.

However, that does raise a good question: was Judas clearly evil? You can sometimes pick a villain in the movies by how they look – that Cruella de Vil wears the skins of puppies is a pretty big warning light. But as much as it would be fun to imagine, Judas wasn't dressed in all black with a scar across one eye and laughing manically. Judas would have seemed just like all the other disciples. In fact, he may have seemed even better than all the other disciples. He had a position of trust and respect within the Twelve, and he was vocal about

40. I know it would make more sense if his name was Judas of Kariot, but that's not how naming worked. I don't know why; it's not like I write books about this kind of stuff.

things like caring for the poor. As we'll see from this passage in John 12, looking respectable and being good are two very different things.

A controversial anointing

This book might be about the not so smart things Jesus' disciples did, but as you read this story in John, we get to see a wonderful thing that one of his female disciples did. It all went down at the house of Lazarus and his sisters, Mary and Martha. This is the Lazarus Jesus raised from the dead (John 11). He and his sisters were having a meal in Jesus' honour. I can imagine after raising Lazarus from the dead, Jesus would have always eaten for free in that house. If I were Jesus, I'd regularly drop in, making subtle hints about how much I love roast potatoes.

Things at this dinner party would probably have been a bit tense. Everyone knew that the authorities were out to get Jesus. Lazarus, Mary, and Martha would have been concerned for the safety of their friend – especially as he was about to make a trip into Jerusalem, the centre of religious authority where all the power players were out to get him.

During the dinner, while Jesus and his disciples were reclining at the table (that's how they sat at a meal in those days, with their torso facing the table and their feet angled out behind them), Jesus was approached by Mary. Mary took a jar of perfume and poured it over Jesus' feet. The perfume is described as 'pure nard, an expensive perfume' (John 12:3). This was an oil that comes from a plant that grows only in the Himalayas, so it had to travel a long way to make it to that dinner party, which would explain its prohibitive cost. As we find out two verses later, the perfume was worth a year's wages. If it were in Australia today, that bottle of perfume would have been worth about the same as a luxury car! That's a very expensive perfume bottle. I spent $80 on perfume for my wife once, and I thought that was a lot. (I hope she doesn't read this and discover that I didn't spend the equivalent of a Mercedes on her aroma.)

Mary put about half a litre of the perfume on Jesus' feet, and the whole house filled with its fragrance. My wife once smashed a small bottle of her expensive perfume (not the same stuff I bought for her) on our bathroom floor and our whole house smelt beautiful for about a week, so I can easily imagine a pint of nard making a significant impact on the atmosphere.

As Mary poured the perfume on Jesus, she wiped his feet with her hair. Women were expected not to show their hair in public, but Mary was so overwhelmed by her thankfulness to Jesus that she was willing to risk scandalising everyone in the room. This was an act of great love and intimacy. She was a woman who clearly loved Jesus very much, and it's obvious why. He was the one who had raised her beloved brother to life again. You can imagine that might move someone to an act of great extravagance.

Judas, however, saw this and said, 'Why wasn't this perfume sold and the money given to the poor? It was worth a year's wages' (v. 5). This would seem like a pretty reasonable response. He was right. I can think of a lot of better things to do with the best part of $100,000 than pour it on someone's feet. And giving it to people who need it more than Jesus' feet is a good idea – a much godlier use of fiscal resources.

However, Judas didn't really say what he said out of some deep need to care for those less fortunate than him. We're told that, 'He did not say this because he cared about the poor but because he was a thief; as keeper of the money bag, he used to help himself to what was put into it' (v. 6). Judas just wanted money to steal for himself. So while plenty could have gone to helping people in need, he could have got himself a good chunk of that money, too. I reckon he probably justified his stealing as being his commission, or the payment he deserved for giving up everything he did to follow Jesus.

Jesus, however, wasn't having any of Judas' false piety: '"Leave her alone," Jesus replied. "It was intended that she should save this perfume for the day of my burial. You will always have the poor among you, but you will not always have me"' (vv. 7–8). Jesus commended Mary for what she had done for him. She is a beautiful example of what extravagant worship looks like. Whether she knew it or not, her anointing of Jesus pointed to the fact that he was about to die. His death, while looking like the death of criminal, was the act of greatest love. His death rescues us from death. Mary's anointing was more than fitting for the King of the universe who was about to die for the sins of the world. Just as we honour fallen heroes, Mary was honouring Jesus for the sacrifice he was about to make.

When Jesus said 'You will always have the poor among you, but you will not always have me', he wasn't saying that we shouldn't bother helping anyone in need because poverty is inevitable. This is an argument I have sometimes heard. In fact, Jesus' answer assumed that his followers *would* help the poor – he was saying we will always have the poor among us, so we will always have opportunities for blessing others materially. Instead, he's saying that sometimes there are unique situations that need a unique response. Mary's extravagant worship of Jesus was the perfect response to Jesus' extravagant grace. In hindsight, knowing what Jesus went on to do at the cross, which follower of Jesus wouldn't give their most lavish gift in his honour? In Matthew's version of this story, Jesus tells those gathered, 'Truly I tell you, wherever this gospel is preached throughout the world, what she has done will also be told, in memory of her' (Matthew 26:13). I'm glad Jesus' words were true and we're still talking about this disciple's worship today.

Respectability

What stands out to me about Judas in this story is that he certainly doesn't look evil at all. Things would be so much easier if he spent the whole dinner sitting at the back of the room, stroking a cat and playing with a knife. But Judas' response to Mary seemed very reasonable. He seemed like a responsible and respectable member of the community reacting against someone else's reckless behaviour. Judas reflects the response of so much false piety. It's easy to condemn others under the guise of your own righteousness. I'm pretty sure if I had been there, I would have thought to myself, 'Judas has a point!' all the while not doing anything to help the poor myself.

It's easy to fall into the trap of judging others' responses to Jesus and jumping on other people's extravagant behaviour in an effort to make ourselves look better in comparison. I have often looked at the lifestyle of other Christians and judged them. When I was an opinionated young man, I once wrote to a church who seemed to be spending money in ways that I disagreed with. I didn't go to the church, I didn't give to the church, I had no stake in that church whatsoever; I just didn't like what they seemed to be doing. So I sent them an email to complain. They were kind enough to write back and respond very graciously to me despite me sticking my nose in where it didn't belong.

Often, we can fall into the trap of expending a lot of energy trying to police other people's righteousness instead of concerning ourselves with our own hearts. You might remember Jesus' teaching in Matthew 7:3–5 where he tells us that before we try to pull the speck of sawdust out of someone else's eye, we should pull the plank out of our own eye. Doing eye surgery with a plank of wood sticking out of your face is a particularly clumsy and dangerous way to operate. That's why you never see surgeons do it. Only surgeons who have taken the plank out of their eye are allowed to do eye surgery. The medical profession is weirdly discriminatory about that. Similarly, only when we have dealt with our own sin are we able to see clearly and to help others with their sin. Only when we've made a true assessment of our hearts can we humbly help others with theirs, one sinner to another. Judas certainly wasn't doing that, and we should be careful that we don't fall into the same trap. Looking like a good Christian and actually being one can be two very different things.[41]

Matthew and Mark both tell us that it was after this dinner party that Judas went to the chief priests and offered to betray Jesus. They offered him thirty pieces of silver, which was about a month's wages. Not nothing, but nothing compared to the year's wages spent on Jesus that evening in his anointing. Judas may have been a thief, but I don't think he betrayed Jesus for the money. He had given up a lot more than a month's wages to spend the last few years with Jesus.

So why did Judas turn on Jesus? Perhaps Jesus' public rebuke of him at the dinner party was the last straw, but it probably wasn't his whole motivation. Nor was it because he was missing out on money to steal from the purse. While we don't know why Judas did what he did, it was probably fuelled by disillusionment with Jesus and the movement he was leading. Judas may have expected Jesus to be a very different kind of Messiah – a Messiah of power, one who would fight the Romans and set up his followers in seats of power, not one who would talk

---

41. I'm aware that there is no such thing as a 'good Christian'. You're either saved by Jesus, or you're not. There are no levels of 'Christian'. But when I say 'good Christian', I'm guessing you know what I mean. There are people who can look very pious, and there are those people who are actually seeking to follow Jesus.

of death at dinner parties while allowing himself to be scandalously anointed by a woman. That wasn't the revolution he had signed up for. But if that's the case, then why weren't the other disciples in the same boat? Hadn't they all expressed similar sentiments throughout their time of following Jesus?

The other disciples, for all their faults, were willing to accept that what Jesus taught was true and to follow him where he led. For Judas, it seems that by the time it got to this dinner party, he didn't trust Jesus anymore. He wasn't willing to submit himself to Jesus' leadership. He thought he knew better than Jesus, and he was willing to betray Jesus because of that.

However, his wasn't just a mild disagreement with Jesus' leadership style. To turn on him, Judas must have been fiercely hurt by Jesus' leadership. He couldn't just walk away. To him, Jesus was dangerous enough that he must be killed.

Did Judas ever love Jesus? At times he probably thought he did. Earlier in his apprenticeship with Jesus, he may have honestly told you that he was a devoted follower of Jesus. After all, he had given everything he had to follow Jesus – just like all the other disciples. But somewhere along the way Judas moved from being a devoted disciple, to disillusioned, to an outright traitor.

Judas, you, and me

The sobering thought for me is that I'm sure Judas appeared like any of the other disciples. When Jesus sent out the Twelve to heal and cast out demons

(Mark 6:6–13), there's no indication that Judas didn't fully participate. When Jesus mentioned that one of his disciples was a devil (John 6:70–71), there's no suggestion that all the disciples looked at Judas, noticed his little horns, and said to each other, 'Oh that makes sense.' Later, at the Last Supper, when Jesus told the disciples that one of them would betray him, they all said, 'Surely you don't mean me?' (Mark 14:19), rather than, 'Surely you mean Judas, Lord. Look at his shifty eyes and snakeskin pants.' The person who turned their back on Jesus looked like everyone else. And today, the one who commits terrible evil can seem like your average, everyday citizen.

Perhaps this scares you. What if you turn out to be a Judas? How can you tell what's going to happen to your heart? To you I would say this: I don't know your heart, but the choice is yours. If you love and trust Jesus, you aren't a Judas, and you won't be a Judas. Hold fast to Jesus, seeking to obey and follow him wherever he leads you. If you do this, you won't suddenly become a traitor, but more and more you will become like the Jesus you follow because you'll see that the Holy Spirit is holding fast to you. Judas chose his path, and you can choose yours too.[42]

---

42. I know some of you are stressing out about predestination right now. Yes, God predestines us, but he also allows us to make our own decisions and holds us accountable for them. Somehow God's sovereignty and our choices are both true facts of the Bible. How? To answer that is too much for a footnote. But you're welcome to check out my YouTube video on the subject that I referenced before by searching 'twfrench predestination'. It may not fully answer the

A question that often comes up is, 'Did Judas go to hell?' Judas has been somewhat romanticised over the years. He's portrayed as a tragic rather than evil character. I think this is because of how his life ended. After he betrayed Jesus we're told that Judas 'was seized with remorse and returned the thirty pieces of silver to the chief priests and the elders. "I have sinned," he said, "for I have betrayed innocent blood"' (Matthew 27:3–4).

The priests were unwilling to accept any responsibility, or look after their traitor, so Judas, unable to find solace, threw the money into the temple, left, and hanged himself. The priests did not keep Judas' money because it was blood money, so instead they bought a field in which to bury foreigners (Matthew 27:5–10).

The problem for Judas in the end was not the terrible crime he had committed – that could be forgiven. Jesus' death was sufficient to gain Judas forgiveness, even for his betrayal, if only he would have looked to God for forgiveness. But he couldn't see how he could be forgiven for what he had done, so just as he took matters into his own hands when he handed Jesus over to the religious authorities, he repeated his mistake and took matters into his own hands when he killed himself. His suicide did not condemn him to hell – that is a lie that has been perpetuated, which is very unhelpful. His inability to trust in Jesus is what brought his condemnation; Judas

issue, but I'm not sure predestination was ever meant to be fully understandable.

could not trust Jesus, not in life and not in death. He was attempting to pay for his own sin, rather than seeking God's mercy. But trying to pay for your own sin will never be sufficient. We need Jesus for that.

So Judas received the punishment his sins deserved. Jesus tells the disciples at the Last Supper: 'Woe to that man who betrays the Son of Man! It would be better for him if he had not been born' (Matthew 26:24). In Acts, Judas' treachery is described as wickedness (Acts 1:18). The Bible has nothing good to say about Judas. He is a warning to us all.

It might be a good time here to mention, seeing as we're talking about pretty dark stuff, that if you feel depressed, or are even thinking about taking your own life, you can and should get help. You might be feeling despair about your own sin, or you might feel like God is against you. Know this: God is not against you. God's love is more that we can even comprehend. If Jesus shows us anything, it is that God is all-in for us. No matter how you feel, the reality of God's love is unchangeable. I'm not expecting that my few words will change things; your distress may be attached to something completely different to your feelings about your sin and God's love. Whatever it is that is making you feel the way you do, there are people who can help you. Wherever you are, google 'depression helpline' and the name of your country or state, and there will be people who you can talk to and who can help you. They won't judge you – they really are only there to help.

Judas clearly felt a desperate remorse about his betrayal of Jesus, but he didn't realise that even after such treachery he could have been forgiven. God's love for Judas did not waver, but Judas, who would not trust Jesus in life, could not trust him at the moment when he clearly saw his own sin. Judas was so overwhelmed by regret that he could not believe in God's love for him.

We cannot base our belief in the power of God's love on our feelings about ourselves or our sin. It isn't easy when we feel terrible and know we have failed God and hurt others, but we need to cling to the fact of the mercy and love of God. If there is a deepest truth in the universe, it is the love of God. We know this for sure because we see it in Jesus. The death to which Judas handed Jesus over is the death that is sufficient to absorb any punishment. That is enough, and that is everything.

Let me just reiterate, if you are feeling depressed, are thinking about harming yourself, or considering taking your own life, there is help available. In Australia you can call Kids Help Line (1800 555 1800), Lifeline (13 11 14), or Beyond Blue (1300 22 4636), or google them and you can chat to them online. If you're not in Australia, google 'Depression Help' and your country or state name and you should find resources. If you or someone you know is in immediate danger, call 000 in Australia or whatever the number is for emergency services in your country.

11

'JESUS, DO YOU WANT TO JOIN OUR TRINITY?'

James and John's Request
Mark 10:32-45

I like to think of myself as someone who can generally make good decisions, like not investing all my life savings in Blockbuster Video, and only rarely falling for scam phone calls from foreign numbers. But every now and again I misread a situation and make bad choices. I have been known to pull a prank or two. Done well, pranks are fun for everyone involved. Done badly, they're no fun for anyone, especially not the person being pranked, but the pranker can feel bad too.

At a youth group that I used to run, we would sometimes have these big events where we'd all get together on a Saturday night. We'd have games, food, an air hockey machine, a band, and a visiting speaker. We would deck out the church with special lighting and have a theme for everyone to dress up as. We called these events 'Ernie's Big Night' because our youth group was called Ernie.[43]

One Ernie's Big Night my co-youth minister and I decided to play a prank on our youth group. During the prayer time we decided to announce to the group that we'd just received some shocking news that the pastor of our church had been involved in a car accident. I know that's not a funny prank, but we said that it had been a crash with a marshmallow truck. We decided to make a lot of marshmallow jokes, which we thought would make it clear that it wasn't true. 'The car has been covered in marshmallows, it's now an Iced Volvo.'[44] 'He's currently in a very sticky situation.' 'Emergency workers have told us that he's in good spirits and enjoying licking his wounds.'

We thought these jokes were very funny. Unfortunately, we played it all straight and not all the kids in our youth group realised we were joking. Some were very upset, one or two may have started crying,

43. I know Ernie is a strange name for a youth group, but so is Resolve, or Energise, or Powerhouse, or all the other names that youth groups have. The youth group I lead at the moment is called Inner North Youth Group, which isn't a very exciting name, but at least you can tell what it is from the name.

44. If you're not Australian, Iced Vovos are a sweet biscuit or cookie which consist of a biscuit topped with jam, marshmallow, and coconut. I stole this pun off a morning radio presenter.

and others were very angry at us for making light of a terrible event. It took a bit of work to convince them that the whole thing was made up. We had to apologise for our bad reading of the situation. We should have known that when you're in a position of authority, your words carry a different weight than they do when you're just hanging with your mates.[45]

Misreading a situation and making light of a terrible, made-up event is one stupid thing to do. Chances are you can think of times when you've misjudged a situation and said or done something inappropriate too. However, we're about to look at something James and John did which was a lot worse. They didn't make jokes about a fake event – they decided to use a real, impending tragedy to secure a better life for themselves. Come on guys, read the room!

Bad request, try again

Jesus and the disciples were on their way to Jerusalem, and once again Jesus had pulled his disciples aside and told them about what was coming up for him: his imminent arrest, humiliation, torture, death, and resurrection (Mark 10:32–34). As we've noted before, whenever Jesus did this his disciples had some compulsive need to go and do something stupid. It's like the writers of the Bible wanted us to clearly see

45. If you're reading this and you were at Ernie's Big Night, once again, I'm sorry. We should have read the room better. Also, send me an email and let me know what you're up to! I'd love to hear from you.

how difficult it was for the disciples to get their heads around Jesus' true mission.

So what did they do this time?

Well, James and John came up to Jesus and asked him this question: '"Teacher," they said, "we want you to do for us whatever we ask"' (v. 35).

Sometimes when people ask me 'Can you do me a favour?' I say 'Sure!' Which is very dangerous, because who knows what they are going to ask me? They might want me to give them a high-five, or they might want me to pledge to them my firstborn child. And then I'd have to do it because I've already said 'Sure!'

Jesus, however, was very smart. He did something we can all learn from. He responded: 'What do you want me to do for you?' (v. 36). Jesus wasn't going to be tricked into agreeing to something before he knew what it was. Jesus is a nice guy, but he didn't easily fall into traps by being overly friendly. That's a mistake reserved for people like me.

James and John made their request: 'Let one of us sit at your right and the other at your left in your glory' (v. 37).

Now let's just consider this request for a little bit. Jesus had just told them that he was going to die. It's a bit like if your friend told you that they had cancer. If you get news like this, your first response should be something like, 'Oh no! I'm so sorry to hear that. Please let me know if there's anything I can do for you.' The wrong first response would be something along the lines of, 'Oh. Does that mean you might not be using your Xbox anymore?'

That is about the level of insensitivity of James and John. To be fair, I'm not sure they had really registered exactly what Jesus was saying, though it's hard to see how Jesus could have been any clearer. It wasn't as if he was talking in vague euphemisms. He was pretty clear: 'mock... spit... flog... kill... rise' (v. 34).

James and John seem to have understood that Jesus was their Messiah King, but they couldn't grasp that this involved Jesus' torture and death; they had only seen a chance to seize power in his kingdom. They figured they were on their way to Jerusalem, the capital city, with the Messiah – it was time to secure themselves some plum jobs.

Jesus said to them, 'You don't know what you are asking' (v. 38). Which was true, they had no idea. They were expecting Jesus to rock up in Jerusalem, kick out the Romans, sit down on a throne as king, and rule all of Israel. They wanted thrones with Jesus! They couldn't have got it more wrong. Jesus' throne isn't on earth; it's in heaven. And who does the Bible say is at God's right hand? It's Jesus! (Acts 2:32–33; 1 Peter 3:21–22). This means that whoever wanted to sit at Jesus' left hand was trying to take the place of God the Father! That was definitely not a spot that either James or John could fill, no matter how impressive they were. People were amazed when a reality television star wanted to become President of the United States. This is much worse.

Jesus continued with his questioning, 'Can you drink the cup I drink or be baptised with the baptism I am baptised with?' (v. 38).

These two didn't miss a beat: 'We can' (v. 39).

James and John fell into the same trap that they set for Jesus. They agreed to something without knowing what it was. They expected that they were able to do the tasks that were in front of Jesus without even knowing what they were. They just clicked 'Yes' on the terms and conditions without reading them. This is dangerous behaviour, even though we all do it. I've agreed to so many terms and conditions, I'm worried that one day some Russians are going to turn up at my door and ship me off to Siberia so they can perform strange medical experiments on me just because I didn't read the terms and conditions on some app that gave me fake muscles in all my photos. On the upside, strange medical experiments gone wrong is how you might become a superhero, so it may not be all bad.

What had James and John signed up for? Jesus said to them, 'You will drink the cup I drink and be baptised with the baptism I am baptised with, but to sit at my right or left is not for me to grant. These places belong to those for whom they have been prepared' (vv. 39–40). For Jesus, the cup that he was talking about was the cup of God's wrath that was before him, which he spoke about in the Garden of Gethsemane before he died (Mark 14:36). The baptism was probably a metaphor for death, where Jesus would go down into the grave and then rise again – just as Paul used baptism as a metaphor for death and resurrection (Romans 6:1–3). Jesus was saying to James and John, 'You will die, just like me.' This was not the answer they were hoping for; they had completely misread the situation. They wanted to rule in power, but they had accidentally agreed to die a violent death. James would go on to be the first of the apostles martyred, and John is said to have been tortured, boiled alive, and left for dead on an island.[46] Following Jesus would not give them the positions of power they had hoped for.

Next, we read that the other disciples heard about James and John's inappropriate request and got upset, presumably because of James and John's selfish audacity, so Jesus decided that it was probably the right time to give them a little bit of teaching on what it means to follow him, and how one might become great.

How to be great

If I were to ask you to name the great people of history, who would you name? Queen Victoria? Cleopatra?

---

46. The idea that John was boiled alive (and survived!) comes from the ancient Christian writer Tertullian. It may have been a legendary account to show John survived martyrdom. When Jesus says John will drink the cup he drinks, he may not have meant that John will die a violent death like he did, but could be referring to John's suffering as he was exiled on the island of Patmos. Sean McDowell, *The Fate of the Apostles: Examining the Martyrdom Accounts of the Closest followers of Jesus* (Abingdon: Routledge, 2016), 150.

Winston Churchill? JFK? Steve Irwin? Ruth Bader Ginsburg?

If I were to ask you how to become great, what would you say? Get elected to political office? Earn a lot of money? Become an influencer?

When I was a boy, I was sure that my path to greatness was through an impressive acting career. I was going to be a famous action movie hero. I was planning to have huge muscles and excellent fighting skills, earn millions of dollars, and sign thousands of autographs. It was going to be fantastic! Unfortunately, my acting chops didn't match up to my imagination chops, so I gave up on that dream. Somewhere in mid-high school I replaced that dream with one of becoming a famous action movie director, and the cycle began again.

Whatever your dreams for greatness are, the good news is, Jesus is about to tell us the secret to becoming great. This is actually great! Unfortunately, his recipe for success does not involve being rich, or famous, or flying anywhere in a private jet.

Following James and John's inappropriate suggestion that they might be able to be on Jesus' senior leadership team, Jesus turned to all the disciples and gave them this teaching on how to be great: 'You know that those who are regarded as rulers of the Gentiles lord it over them, and their high officials exercise authority over them. Not so with you. Instead, whoever wants to become great among you must be your servant, and whoever wants to be first must be slave of all. For even the Son of Man did not come to be served, but to serve, and to give his life as a ransom for many' (Mark 10:42–45).

How can you be great? It isn't by having the ability to push people around or having people look after your every whim. It also isn't by having lots of people know who you are, or admire your wealth, brains, talent, or looks. You become great by serving. Jesus isn't saying the path to greatness is *through* service. He's saying that greatness *is* service.

Who do you think is greater: the person who orders food to be delivered, or the person who delivers the food? In Jesus' equation it's the person who delivers. (Which actually makes a lot of sense, if you think about it. There is a person who magically appears at your door with noodles whenever you want them. They are some kind of underpaid genie!)[47] Who do you think is greater: the one who makes the house dirty, or the one who cleans it? In Jesus' kingdom, it's the cleaner. How do we know? Because that's what Jesus does. Jesus is the ruler of the universe who could have come to earth and ruled over everyone. He could have demanded food, clothes, palaces, and slaves. But Jesus had no slaves, no palaces, and no home. He came and served – by healing people, befriending the marginalised, speaking up for those who have no voice, feeding multitudes, and teaching us the way to know God. Ultimately, he died naked on a cross, serving humanity. He gave his life as a ransom for ours,

----

47. Seeing as your delivery person is legitimately great, make sure you tip them. I reckon it's what Jesus would do.

becoming a slave to free us from slavery to sin and death, dying so that we might receive new life. When you put it like that, his greatness becomes clear.

So how do you be great? You serve.

Greatness is picking up rubbish. It's helping your brother or sister with their homework. It's helping a friend move house. It's visiting your grandparents on a Saturday. It's unpacking the dishwasher. It's cleaning up someone else's vomit. It's sticking up for someone who is being bullied or harassed. It's doing yard work for someone who can't. It's babysitting for free. It's stacking chairs at church even when your crush isn't looking.

'But that's no fun!' I hear you say. Yeah, on paper it doesn't look fun at all, but here's the secret I've discovered: serving never looks fun on the outside. But sometimes, when you actually do it, it feels great. (And sometimes it's just hard work, no one notices, and you're tempted to feel like people are just taking advantage of your kindness.)

Have you ever heard someone say, 'You should do this, it'll look great on your CV'? When you're in high school, it starts to become a standard phrase. 'You should volunteer for this… You should sign up for that… It'll look great on your résumé.' As if all of life is about helping get that first job at McDonald's (which looks great on your résumé, by the way). There is nothing wrong with résumé building. But don't pretend that volunteering at the local retirement village two hours a week or collecting money for a charity at a train station one day of the year so that you can show some job interviewer you have community spirit is a great act of service (except perhaps self-service). Greatness comes from service that is not self-centred but comes from a desire to help others.

It's the same if you volunteer for something just because your crush is there. I mean, go for it! I'm all for doing a good deed for a good flirt. But once again, don't pretend you're a good person because you kindly pick up rubbish next to that person you like for an hour if you would never pick up rubbish if they weren't there.

'I want to serve others, but when I do, I'm also thinking about my CV, and about impressing the person that I like, and hoping my parents are happy with me! My motivations are all wrong. I'll never be great!'

It's true that our motivations can be wrong. Sometimes I get the chance to preach to people, and whenever I get up there, I have many different motivations. Of course I'm hoping that people hear the good news of Jesus and learn how to love and serve him better. But I'm also thinking about how I want people to laugh at my jokes. I'm hoping people will think I'm an impressive man of God.[48]

The saying goes, if you wait for your motivations to be right, you'll never do anything. This is true. We're always going to wrestle with mixed motivations. Our pride and selfishness will battle with our desire to do

---

48. When I was single, I would also hope that single women would see me preach and be so impressed they'd want to date me. Then one day that actually happened, and now I'm married to her, so that sermon worked out pretty well – at least for me.

what is right. So sometimes the answer is just to get on with whatever it is that you're meant to be doing and trust that your motivations will catch up. It's not as if everything you do with the wrong motivation is going to be useless – God can use our service even if our motivation is impure. God is not going to condemn you to hell because you wanted to serve Jesus but were also keen to eat the free cookies at leadership meetings.

Imagine if when you were learning to walk, you took your first steps, and then when you fell over your parents were like, 'This is terrible. Useless. If you can't walk properly you won't walk at all. We're going to carry you everywhere for the rest of your life, like a baby.'

Or if you told your parents you like brushing your teeth because you like the taste of toothpaste, and they said, 'What?! You have terrible motivation. Toothbrushing is for dental hygiene, not for fun!' And you weren't allowed to brush your teeth again.

Of course, you get better at walking, or whatever you do, the more you do it. Just as you learn the importance of dental hygiene even if you don't continue to love the taste of toothpaste, if you start something for the wrong reasons, you can learn the right reasons as you go.

Get started, and you'll get better at it as you go. Ask for help. Tell people your struggles. Try new roles. Pray. Keep working at it and asking Jesus to change your heart, and he will.

But other times, when you know your motivations are totally off, the best thing you can do is quit.

'What? Quit?' Yeah. Quit. Imagine you've always wanted to be a worship leader. It's been your dream forever. It's like the Christian version of being a rock star. You start learning to play guitar. You follow all the biggest worship leaders on Instagram. You get vocal training. You start playing in the band. Finally, you get the chance to lead at a youth event one night. You start planning your outfit, your Instagram posts. You are thinking about how impressed everyone is going to be when they see how well you play guitar and hear how well you sing. When you get to do it, it feels great! Everyone is singing along, you're feeling the vibes, the lighting is great, the band is on fire. When you get off stage everyone tells you what a great job you did, and while you're humble on the outside, in your brain you can't help but agree with them.

Or imagine you've been asked to lead a Bible study group. You're not sure what to expect, but you say you'll give it a go. The night before the group you go through all your notes. Then you get there and start leading the group and people ask you about some passage in the Bible, you tell them what you think, and they all seem very impressed with your answers. It feels really good. They ask more questions, you give more answers, they just seem to love everything you have to say – and you love them loving everything you have to say. Every week from then on, you can't wait for Bible study group so that you can share all your wisdom and have all those people listen to all your wisdom.

In both of these scenarios you're definitely serving, but your motivation is a lot more about you than about those who you are helping. You want to be impressive, to have people looking at you or hanging on your every word. In these situations, when it's clear that your motivation is coming almost entirely from the wrong place, perhaps the best thing you can do is quit. There's a good chance it's the only way you can fix your broken view of why you're serving. But if you do quit your role, don't just disappear. Find somewhere else to serve. Move chairs or help out in the sound booth. Volunteer to cook meals for the Bible study group. Don't stop serving, just stop serving your ego.

After a while, maybe months, maybe years, you may feel like your heart is in the right place to begin serving again in the ministry you quit. Perhaps then it would be a good idea to chat to someone older and wiser, see if they agree, and help you be accountable for your motivations. When the time is right and you go back to serving, you will be all the better at worship leading, Bible study facilitating, or whatever else it is you do, if you have first learned to get you heart in check.

So how does someone go about getting their motivations right? I think this is an important time to learn the gospel again. In fact, whether your motivations are good or not, it's always a good time to re-learn the gospel. It's the only way to learn true servanthood.

Jesus could have just told us to be servants, but instead he lived it out. He didn't come to be served but to serve. The greatest example of servant leadership that Jesus gave us was himself, when he gave his life in exchange for ours. We cultivate a servant attitude by looking to the greatest servant: Jesus! This is why Paul wrote Philippians 2 the way he did. When the Philippians needed to be encouraged to look out for the interests of others before themselves, he didn't say do it because it's the right thing to do, he said:

> In your relationships with one another, have the same mindset as Christ Jesus:
>> who, being in very nature God,
>>> did not consider equality with God
> something to be used to his own advantage;
>> rather, he made himself nothing
>>> by taking the very nature of a servant,
>>> being made in human likeness.
> And being found in appearance as a man,
>> he humbled himself
>>> by becoming obedient to death –
>>>> even death on a cross!
>
> Therefore God exalted him to the highest place and gave him the name that is above every name, that at the name of Jesus every knee should bow, in heaven and on earth and under the earth, and every tongue acknowledge that Jesus Christ is Lord, to the glory of God the Father. (Philippians 2:5–11)

Our motivation for service is the great service of our servant King. It's the good news of what Jesus has done for us that will change our hearts daily, so we know that it's not about us, but about the one who has saved us. That is why we continue to spend time in his Word and meeting with him, so that we might understand his love for us, and live that life for others. That's a lesson that James and John ended up learning, serving Jesus with their whole lives. When we can do that, we'll be truly great.

12

OVERPROMISE, UNDER-DELIVER

Jesus Is Deserted
Matthew 26:31-56

If you heard someone calling out for help in the middle of the night, would you go to help them? Of course you would. You wouldn't leave someone outside in the dark, crying out for someone to help them, while you stayed in your warm bed. If you'd asked me that a few years ago, I would have thought the same. The problem is, as good as I like to think I am, I was once in that exact situation, and I didn't do anything.

I was on holidays with my wife in Tasmania. We were staying in an Airbnb in a suburb of Hobart. Our house was on a long street in a valley, with houses going up the hill on either side. One night, at around 2am, I was awoken by the sound of what seemed to be someone yelling outside. I lay in bed, slowly waking up, trying to make out what I just heard.

'Help!'

There it was again. There was a man outside somewhere in the valley, yelling for help. At this point in time, I wish I'd jumped out of bed, threw on some clothes, and said, 'Someone needs my help!' – like some kind of superhero. But what I actually did was lay in bed, heart beating, running through all the things that could confront me if I answered the call. Someone who had been stabbed? Someone who had been injured in a car accident? Someone with a hurt friend? None of those situations seemed like things I was equipped to deal with.

'Help me! Someone help me!'

'Okay,' I thought, 'what would Jesus do?' He'd help, of course he would. 'Then you better help, Tom! Get out of bed and go help that man!' Heart beating even harder, I was scared to get out of bed.

'Help me! Please! Someone!'

'I'm doing it! I'm getting out of bed. I'm going to the bathroom, and then I'm putting my clothes on, then I'm going to help that guy.' I got out of bed, I did an epic wee, and then I stood near the front door in my pyjamas listening for the man.

I heard him. And he was yelling. But he wasn't yelling for help anymore. He was swearing. Swearing at everyone. His voice got louder as he got closer to our place. Dropping F bombs, and all the other bombs, in that dark Tasmanian street.

'Phew!' I thought. 'I don't have to help him.' I went back to bed, my adrenaline still pumping. As I lay in bed (next to my wife who had slept soundly through the whole thing), I wondered what had happened. I assumed he was drunk, wandering home from the pub. Maybe he was yelling because he wanted a lift home. Or maybe he was actually in trouble. Just because you're drunk, doesn't mean you're not in trouble. In fact, you're a lot more likely to get into trouble if you're drunk. Perhaps he had broken his arm or had got into a fight and was injured. I don't know. I assume that the swearing in the street indicated that things weren't as bad as his cries for help had first implied, but I wasn't to know that when he first started calling out.

For days I could hear his cries in my head. I can still recall them now, when I think about it. As good as I like to think I am, someone needed my help, and I didn't answer the call.

I wonder if you've had times like I did. When your view of yourself and your own goodness is starkly confronted with what you actually do in the moment.

As we've gone on our journey with the disciples, we've seen them disappoint in many different ways. But perhaps there was no time when the gap between their self-perceived faithfulness and their actual cowardly actions was more clearly displayed than in the final twenty-four hours before Jesus was killed. Their friend and leader was in deep trouble, but none of them responded in the way they would have hoped. They boldly (but naively) committed themselves to Jesus to the point of death, only to be exposed as cowards hours later. For these eleven men, their world was turned upside down – showing them with absolute clarity who they really were.

Night in the garden

Everything began when Jesus held a Passover meal with his disciples. The Passover was a feast that the Jews held every year, when they remembered the time that God rescued them from the rule of the Egyptians. God sent a number of plagues, including frogs, hail, gnats, boils, and darkness, all culminating in the death of the firstborn male in every family in Egypt. The Israelites were told to smear their door frames with the blood of a lamb so that God would pass over their houses and spare their sons. They were protected from the judgement of God by the blood of the lamb. (You can read all about the events of that first Passover in Exodus 1–12.)

Every year, the Jews would commemorate this with a feast, retelling the story of the time God rescued them from slavery. This is the ceremony that Jesus held with his disciples on the night before he was killed.

During the evening, Jesus reimagined the Passover meal to commemorate a new kind of saving that God was going to do. Jesus handed the disciples bread and wine and told them that these things were his body and blood:

> While they were eating, Jesus took bread, and
> when he had given thanks, he broke it and

gave it to his disciples, saying, 'Take and eat; this is my body.'

Then he took a cup, and when he had given thanks, he gave it to them, saying, 'Drink from it, all of you. This is my blood of the covenant, which is poured out for many for the forgiveness of sins. I tell you, I will not drink from this fruit of the vine from now on until that day when I drink it new with you in my Father's kingdom.' (Matthew 26:26–29)

Jesus was teaching his twelve disciples to reframe the Passover. No longer would they only remember the blood of the lamb that saved Israel from God's judgement on Egypt; they would now remember that Jesus shed his blood to save them from God's wrath against all of humanity's sin. Jesus was showing them that the Passover was not only about remembering what God did in Egypt, it was also pointing to the work that Jesus was going to do at the cross. God was making a new, ultimate promise with humanity to finally, and fully, save us from our sins and to bring us into a new kingdom through the work of Jesus, the true Passover lamb.

After the meal they all got up and went for a walk out of the city. On the way, Jesus told them something they thought was unbelievable – that they would all abandon him: 'This very night you will all fall away on account of me, for it is written: "I will strike the shepherd, and the sheep of the flock will be scattered."

But after I have risen, I will go ahead of you into Galilee' (Matthew 26:31–32).

Peter, always optimistic about his own abilities (remember when he decided walking on water would be a cinch?), was having none of it. He had no doubts about his undying commitment to Jesus. He told Jesus, 'Even if all fall away on account of you, I never will' (v. 33).

But Jesus knew better than Peter and promised him, 'Truly I tell you... this very night, before the cock crows, you will disown me three times' (v. 34).

Peter, never afraid to disagree with Jesus, responded, 'Even if I have to die with you, I will never disown you' (v. 35). And all the other disciples insisted the same.

Here we can see the bravado of the disciples. They were sure that, faced with the worst, most difficult moment of their lives, they would not give up on Jesus – they would stick by him, no matter what.

On their arrival at the Garden of Gethsemane Jesus left most of the group to pray alone, taking with him only Peter, James, and John. He shared with them of his grief about what was approaching: 'My soul is overwhelmed with sorrow to the point of death. Stay here and keep watch with me' (v. 38).

Leaving the three behind, Jesus went a little deeper into the garden and cried out to God in anguish. He said, 'My Father, if it is possible, may this cup be taken from me. Yet not as I will, but as you will' (v. 39). Jesus knew he was about to experience the most terrible pain. Not just the pain of torture and crucifixion, but the infinitely worse pain of bearing the sin of humanity; being cut off from his Father on our behalf. After having an eternally perfect relationship, he was about to feel the infinite gap between God and a sinner. If you think about how much it hurts when someone you love is angry with you, imagine that pain. Between Jesus and his Father, who had loved each other since before the creation of the world, the experience would have been indescribably more devastating.

As Jesus returned to his disciples, he found them sleeping. The very same people who, just a little while earlier, had promised to die with Jesus could not even stay awake with him.

I can't imagine how disappointing this must have been for Jesus. I assume the disciples also felt terrible, but not terrible enough to stay awake, because we're told that this happened twice more. This was not just a one-off mistake. The disciples' inability to stay awake with Jesus exposed a significant flaw in their faithfulness. Perhaps you know how this feels? When the gap between what you want to do and what you actually do is laid bare. When you promise something, only to fail to live up to your promises almost immediately.

The inability of the disciples to stay awake with Jesus was a harbinger of the abandonment that was to come. When Jesus found them sleeping for a third time, he said, 'Are you still sleeping and resting? Look, the hour has come, and the Son of Man is delivered into the hands of sinners. Rise! Let us go! Here comes my betrayer!' (v. 45–46). Here was Judas, about to commit an act that Jesus had prophesied about on many occasions.

Judas arrived with a large crowd. They were guards from the temple (think Church Police – which is a terrifying thought) and perhaps a few extras. They had weapons, including swords and wooden clubs. As they came to arrest Jesus, they were ready to deal with any opposition. But they came in the middle of the night, because they knew arresting Jesus in broad daylight could have caused a riot. When authorities begin enacting 'justice' in secret, there is a good chance their justice is not just at all.

Judas, leading the guards, knew where Jesus and the rest of the disciples would be. He approached Jesus and kissed him. While in Western culture we're not so likely to greet others with kisses, in Bible times it was pretty common, so to an outsider watching, nothing would have seemed out of the ordinary. What was important was who Judas was kissing. The guards didn't have photos to compare Jesus' face against to identify him, and in the secret of the dark, Jesus and the disciples would have all looked similar. Judas did his job and with one kiss identified exactly who Jesus was.

Jesus knew exactly what was happening, and he said to Judas, 'Do what you came for, friend' (v. 50), and with that, Jesus was seized. The book of John tells us that Peter was so incensed by this that, being the impulsive guy that he was, he grabbed his sword and chopped off the ear of one of the men who had come to arrest Jesus. John also tells us the earless guy's name was Malchus, just in case you want to look him up next time you're in ancient Israel (John 18:10).

I'm not a particularly violent guy, but I feel like I know a few people who would do exactly the same thing as Peter. His determination to protect Jesus is admirable, especially considering he was up against pretty bad odds – he was taking on a whole crowd of armed men. I also suspect that Peter wasn't actually that good at fighting. For one, he was a fisherman, and fish don't often fight back. Also, the fact that he chopped off the guy's ear seems like it was a mistake. I doubt he was going for the ear – he probably just missed the rest of the head.

Either way, Jesus wasn't impressed: '"Put your sword back in its place," Jesus said to him, "for all who draw the sword will die by the sword. Do you think I cannot call on my Father, and he will at once put at my disposal more than twelve legions of angels? But how then would the Scriptures be fulfilled that say it must happen in this way?"' (Matthew 26:52–54).

Once he had said this, we are told in Luke that Jesus then reached out and healed the guy's ear (Luke 22:51). This is pretty impressive! When I drive, I refuse to let people into traffic if they've pushed in, and here's Jesus, who is so full of love that he heals a guy who was attempting to arrest him so he might be put to death.

Like Peter, it's not uncommon for followers of Jesus to make bad decisions when attempting to defend Jesus. You only have to hang out online a bit to see Christians attacking those who don't follow Jesus, in an attempt to defend him. But Jesus doesn't need us to defend him. As he says to Peter, he has twelve legions of angels (around 60,000 angels) at his disposal if he wants them. While I personally would like to see 60,000 fiery messengers of death turn up on some YouTube troll's doorstep, Jesus isn't as petty as I am. We need to look at how Jesus defends himself: not with violence or abuse, but with love, gentleness, and truth. From his arrest to his execution, Jesus never once sought to harm those who attacked him. Instead, he spoke with respect, and even prayed for the men who were executing him (Luke 23:34). The result of this was that people who watched Jesus as he died chose to put their faith in him (Luke 23:39–43, 47).

As we respond to people attacking us or our faith, our job is not to retaliate and defend Jesus. Instead, like him, we need to love with grace in the hopes that by our love, they too might put their faith in him.

It's amazing that the calmest, most rational person at Jesus' arrest was the guy getting arrested. The disciples, on the other hand, all 'deserted him and fled' (Matthew 26:56).[49] The same guys who promised they would die

---

49. In Mark 14:51–52 we are also told there was a nude guy streaking at Jesus' arrest, trying to escape getting caught with him. I'm sure that was pretty disappointing for Jesus. Not only had his friends left him, but there was one guy who was so afraid of being associated with Jesus that he was willing to be caught nude in the street. I've written a lot more about this weird part of the Bible in my book, *Weird, Crude, Funny, and Nude: The Bible Exposed* (2018), which you're obviously welcome to read for some deep theological truths about ancient streakers.

with Jesus left him all alone. Perhaps when Jesus shut down Peter's violence, they had no idea how they should respond. If Jesus had been arrested and they couldn't fight and die for him, what other options did they have? If Jesus wouldn't defend himself, perhaps he had given up. Should they just quit too? Or perhaps the most obvious answer is the right one: they were just afraid that they too would be arrested with Jesus. Despite all their bravado, they were not really willing to die with him at all.

Jesus is not surprised

I don't know what this story does for you, but for me it highlights some of the most painful aspects of following Jesus. How often do we fail to live up to our own desires for fidelity? Sometimes we sing songs at church declaring our undying faithfulness to Jesus, only to find within hours that we haven't lived up to the words we have just sung. I can remember times when I would pray to God at church, committing my life to him, only to find myself looking at porn that very night. Sin stings worse when you can so easily contrast who you pretend to be with the person who you want to be.

Perhaps at times like this you imagine Jesus being angry and disappointed. Perhaps you worry that at some point Jesus is going to give up on you because of the sin that you continually disavow and continually come back to. It may feel like there will come a time when Jesus will just decide that you've had too many chances and he's done with you.

199

But what do we see in Jesus' behaviour in the garden? While the disciples promised that they would never leave Jesus, he knew they would do exactly that. In fact, it had been prophesied hundreds of years before (see Matthew 26:31). As disappointing as the disciples' inability to live up to their promises was, Jesus never expected them to stick by him. He knew he was going to the cross alone, and he still chose to do it. God's grace is entirely reliant on his kindness to us, not our ability to keep our promises to him.

We can take a lot of comfort knowing that Jesus is not surprised by our sin. He knows our hearts a lot better than we do. So we can rest assured that he isn't going to give up on us. Just as Jesus continued to the cross despite the failures of the disciples, when he called you to himself, he wasn't ever unsure if he was going to keep loving you.

Of course, this doesn't mean that God is unconcerned with our sin. All it means is that our sin doesn't deter him from his mission to rescue us. It was our sin that sent him to the cross. Ephesians 1:4 tells us that we were chosen in Christ to be made holy and blameless before the world was created. If God knew us before he had created the world, then he knew everything there is to know about us. He is not surprised by our sin, and he didn't make a mistake in saving us.

Doesn't this set you free? Not free to sin, but free from the pressure of trying to keep God on side – free from hating yourself for not being perfect. There is nothing you need to prove to God to make him love you. And there is nothing you will do that he hasn't anticipated. Knowing you perfectly, Jesus died for you and called you to salvation. You're never outside of God's love and forgiveness, which means you're free to live the way he calls you to live. When you get it wrong, his grace is there for you. And when you get right, it's a testament to the Holy Spirit at work in you.

Jesus was arrested and went to the cross alone. When his disciples abandoned him, he knew exactly who he was saving. He was saving his disappointing disciples, his hateful executioners, his abusive onlookers, and people like you and me – who would also overpromise obedience only to under-deliver time and again. He died for all of us, knowing who we are and what we would do, so that all of us who would put our trust in him might become children of God.

Jesus, knowing he would be abandoned, went to the cross so that we would know that he will never abandon us.

13

CALLING DOWN CURSES

Peter Denies Jesus
John 18:15-27

You know that feeling when you say a stupid thing, and as soon as the words come out of your mouth, you realise you're in trouble? You can't get those words back, and you may never live them down. I feel like that happens to me on a semi-regular basis.

When I was making my film with Sven from Sweden (who I told you about in Chapter 8), I said a stupid thing. Well, I probably said lots of stupid things, but one thing stands out as particularly foolish. The film I was making was a mocumentary, and there was a scene where my production crew were going to be caught on film. We'd borrowed a boom microphone from school

– we were very professional, don't you know – and my friend Howie (who was also my future housemate, who almost made me die of chicken) was acting as boom operator. For some reason, I thought that Howie looked too much like a school student to be taken seriously as a professional boom guy in my film. So I decided to recast him for my friend Ryan in the pivotal scene. Ryan was a year older than us and didn't go to school anymore. He also had long blonde hair, which I thought made him look a lot more grown up and professional than Howie.[50]

When I informed Howie of my directorial decision to recast him, I told him it because he was 'not aesthetically pleasing enough'. That is a direct quote from my pretentious, seventeen-year-old self.

Howie, to his credit, graciously gave up his boom mic duties. But he also didn't let me forget that I said he wasn't aesthetically pleasing enough. For years, Howie would say things like, 'Do you mind being seen in the car with me, or am I not aesthetically pleasing?' or, 'It's weird seeing you in that hoodie Tom. I thought it wouldn't be aesthetically pleasing enough for you.'

I'd love to tell you that these days Howie is a male model and has proven he truly is aesthetically pleasing, but he isn't (a male model that is; his aesthetics are

---

50. Small piece of trivia: These days, Howie has a licence to operate a boom lift, which he regularly does in his job as production crew on large-scale live events. He was, it turns out, exactly the kind of person who would be a professional boom operator, just large mechanical booms, not boom microphones.

fine). The best I can do is let you know that for many years people would get Howie and me confused, so we are at least as aesthetically unpleasing as each other. What's more, Ryan and his golden locks never showed up in the finished film, but you can clearly see Howie as an extra in the very scene I tried to kick him out of. And I'll always be remembered as the guy who used the phrase 'not aesthetically pleasing' while kicking one of my best friends out of a scene in a film he was helping me make for free.

What I said was stupid, but it wasn't even the worst thing that's ever come out of my mouth, accidentally or deliberately. There are plenty of things I wish I could take back that unfortunately didn't just result in some light mockery.

We're about to delve into the story of when Peter denied he knew Jesus – when he said something stupid, three times in a row. Perhaps you know what it's like to not own up to your faith in Jesus. Maybe because of things you've said, or because you've stayed quiet when you should have spoken up. Unfortunately, those foolish things we say and do never go away, and we can't take them back. But we have Peter's story to show us that even the things we most regret saying, doing or not doing, do not have to be the end of us. They don't have to define us.

The denial

While in the last chapter we saw that all the disciples deserted Jesus, it turns out that Peter and another disciple (most probably John) didn't entirely desert him.[51] After Jesus was arrested, these two came out from wherever they were hiding and 'followed him at a distance, right into the courtyard of the high priest' (Mark 14:54). Everyone else might have left Jesus, but Peter and John couldn't bring themselves to leave Jesus all by himself. Jesus was taken to a trial before the most powerful religious leaders at the home of the high priest. And this wasn't any old home; it was a palatial mansion where the high priest would have meetings and would only have a short walk to work at the temple.

I was once invited to dinner at the house of the Anglican Archbishop of Sydney. In those days, this was a giant mansion that looked like it was straight out of Batman.[52] I was running late so I felt pretty flustered. Arriving feeling slightly stressed at that impressive building was intimidating enough. I can imagine following your master to the Jewish high priest's residence while he was flanked by perhaps hundreds of burly guards would have been a lot more intimidating.

---

51. We are not sure that John actually was the other disciple, it just seems like a good guess because John refers to himself at other points throughout the Gospel of John as the 'beloved disciple'. It also makes sense because we will eventually see John at the foot of the cross when all the other disciples have disappeared (John 19:25–27). It is possible that John followed Jesus all the way from his arrest to his death.

52. These days the Archbishop lives in a more modest home. But it still functions as a place for meetings and doing the job of running the diocese, so it's not the smallest residence ever constructed. Not that I've ever been invited back for dinner, so I can't know for sure.

We're told that when Peter and John arrived, John was able to go in because the high priest knew who he was. John then put in a good word for Peter and got him into the courtyard too (John 18:15–16). It was kind of like getting into a gig because your friend knows the band, if the band was attempting to murder your Messiah.

Were this an adventure movie, this story would be progressing very differently. John and Peter wouldn't have asked permission to enter; instead they would have knocked out some guards, stolen their uniforms, snuck into the palace, and attempted to rescue Jesus. As they walked through the palace trying to look inconspicuous, they would have been stopped by a commander, who would recognise them as being invaders. Consequently, they would have been forced to knock him out too. Then, guards would have found the slumped commander and blown John and Peter's cover, forcing them to burst into the trial and jump out a window with Jesus under a hail of arrows.

Real life has a way of working out differently. Instead of a daring rescue, Peter and John just walked in the front door. On the way into the courtyard, Peter was questioned by a servant girl, who was probably about twelve or thirteen years old. She asked him, 'You aren't one of this man's disciples too, are you?' (v. 17).

Peter, not showing his previous confidence, denied knowing Jesus. You would think that an adult man, a fisherman, who just a little while earlier had attacked an armed man with his sword and tried to take on a few hundred men by himself, would not have been scared of a young servant girl. But it turns out he was.

Jesus, meanwhile, was also being questioned. He refused to deny himself, his identity as the Messiah, or the things he had said and done. He could easily have given in and saved himself a whole lot of pain. But he would not submit to fear.

Back in the courtyard, warming himself by the fire, Peter was in the middle of his own trial, and his wasn't fairing nearly so well. As he stood around the fire with the servants and officials of the high priest, he was asked, 'You aren't one of his disciples too, are you?' (v. 25). Once again, Peter denied knowing Jesus: 'I am not,' he replied.

Finally, one of the high priest's servants, who was a relative of Malchus (the guy who got his ear chopped off), asked Peter, 'Didn't I see you with him in the garden?' (v. 26). For a third time, Peter denied knowing Jesus. In Mark 14:71 we're told that, 'He began to call down curses, and he swore to them, "I don't know this man you're talking about."' Whether Peter was calling down curses on himself or on Jesus, he was desperate to let people know that he was not at disciple of Jesus.

At that moment, a cock crowed.

Jesus, from his position inside the high priest's house, turned and looked at Peter in the courtyard.

Peter immediately remembered Jesus' words to him: 'Before the cock crows today, you will disown me three times' (Luke 22:61).

Peter ran out of the courtyard and wept.

Every so often in your life, there comes a time when you are so clearly confronted with your sin that you can no longer ignore it, downplay it, or move past it. You have seen yourself for who you truly are, and you are filled with shame. I'm sure right now you are picturing those times – they come to mind a lot easier than many of your other memories.

I would now tell you about a time in my life when I have felt like this, but as I'm sure you feel the same way about your own sin; it's not the kind of thing I really want published in a book.

How amazing that we get this insight into Peter's most terrible moment. How do we know all that we know? I suspect it is partly because it was somewhat public. Jesus had warned Peter in front of all the disciples that it would happen, and John may have been around to see it. But more so, I think we know this story because Peter shared it. He was willing to let his most terrible moment be shared in the biographies of Jesus and his story makes it into all four Gospels.

So why would Peter share this painful memory? Why would Peter allow such an unflattering story to go down in history? The disciples, as they led the early church and the movement that became what we know today as Christianity, did not want to be seen as the saviours, or as divine in any way. They wanted us to see that the only extraordinary person in this story is Jesus. The story of Peter's denial of Jesus is dramatically contrasted with Jesus' refusal to deny his Father, his mission, or his identity. Peter was willing to look terrible so that we might see Jesus' beauty all the more.

You and I can identify with Peter. He isn't a superhero man of faith who never faltered and who always knew what to do. If there is anything we have seen from this book, it's that the disciples were entirely unheroic. As you recall your darkest moments, the things you are most ashamed of, what a gift it is to know that you are not the only one to be confronted by your sin, and you are not the only one in deep need of restoration from your Saviour.

When Jesus looks at you

I am sure that part of what broke Peter as he denied knowing his master was the look that Jesus gave him. What did he see in Jesus' look? What did he assume that Jesus thought of him? I would like to think that all he saw was love, but knowing what we humans are like, I suspect he saw condemnation, like Jesus was saying, 'See Peter, I always knew what you were like. I told you this would happen. You're nothing but a failure.' I don't think Peter saw this because that was what Jesus was communicating, but because we have a tendency to read our own expectations in other people's expressions.

I spend a lot of time preaching, and it's easy to look around the room at everyone's expressions and be sure that many of the people there are judging me. And if I say something controversial, I automatically look at the people who I assume might have a problem with what I have said and assume that they are angry at me. Maybe sometimes they are – in fact, I know that sometimes they are because they tell me. Most of the time, however, they are merely listening, or perhaps not listening but thinking about something entirely different (like a meme they want to make or whether it's racist to only order sweet and sour pork when they eat Chinese food), and I'm just imposing my own insecurities onto their facial expressions. Often, it's the people who I want to impress the most whose expressions I spend the most time trying to decode.

When it comes to our relationship with God, it can be so easy to assume we know what God is thinking of us. As we look at our sin and are disgusted by it, we assume that God is disgusted with us. We can be afraid to come to him in prayer, to be seen by him as we truly are, because we know that we cannot hide from him. We're sure that if we cannot hear from God it's because of his vast disappointment with us, and if we were to hear from him it would only be him telling us everything that is wrong with us.

What was Jesus thinking when he looked at Peter? Of course, we cannot know for sure, but we can certainly make an educated guess. Earlier in Luke's Gospel, during the Last Supper, Jesus spoke to Peter and said this: 'Simon, Simon, Satan has asked to sift all of you as wheat. But I have prayed for you, Simon, that your faith may not fail. And when you have turned back, strengthen your brothers' (Luke 22:31–32).

Jesus knew very well what was about to happen to Peter, but he wasn't writing Peter off; he was praying for him. Jesus had bigger things on his mind that night than Peter's weaknesses, but still Jesus was concerned for him, that his faith might survive the trial that was to come. What's more, Jesus was anticipating that Peter would turn back. Peter's denial of his Lord would not be the end of his faith.

The other thing we know is that, as we discovered in Chapter 12, Jesus knew exactly what he was getting himself into. He was aware that Peter would not stand by him, that he would be sifted like wheat and abandon his master. But still Jesus chose to go willingly to his death because he knew exactly what his death would achieve. He was dying because all people, all men and women, would have their own rejection of God to reckon with. As Jesus looked at Peter, whatever Peter saw, I don't think Jesus was looking with condemnation, but with understanding, compassion, and love. Understanding, because Peter was exactly where Jesus had prophesied he would be. Compassion, because he understood the pain that Peter would feel for his sin. And finally, love, because it was Jesus' love for Peter, for the disciples, and for the world that brought him to that point, and that would propel him all the way to the cross.

So let's come back to you. When God looks at you, what look do you think he is giving you? Does he look with condemnation on your sinfulness? Does he look with anger at your weakness? Is he disappointed that you're back in your sin again? If you have put your trust in Jesus, I can guarantee that he doesn't look at you with condemnation because he made a promise to us in Romans that 'there is now no condemnation for those who are in Christ Jesus' (Romans 8:1). He doesn't look at you like a judge but like a loving father. Romans 8 goes on to tell us that if we have put our trust in Jesus then we have the Holy Spirit, and 'those who are led by the Spirit of God are the children of God. The Spirit you received does not make you slaves, so that you live in fear again; rather, the Spirit you received brought about your adoption to sonship. And by him we cry, "*Abba*, Father"' (Romans 8:14–15).

Do you know the story of the Prodigal Son that Jesus told in Luke 15? The prodigal son came home, after wishing his father dead and squandering his father's wealth, prepared to earn his way back into his father's household through working as a hired hand. Yet, what did the father do? He ran to meet his son, threw his arms around him, welcomed him back into the family, and threw a giant party for him.

Whether you've lived a depraved life or the life of a well-behaved church kid only to find yourself in sin when you should have known better, God looks at you not with disappointment but with the love of a father. A father who wants to hold you in his arms and tell you that everything is all right, everything is taken care of, you aren't going to have to pay for you sins, you are forgiven.

Is there a place for God's anger, his judgement, and his condemnation? Of course there is. Sin is sin, and you can clearly see how much God hates sin by what Jesus went through on the cross. Judgement is

God taking seriously the pain inflicted on his creation because of sin – God's judgement is a consequence of his love. Sadly, if you haven't put your trust in Jesus, then you will not know God as Father, and you will meet him only as judge. But the choice is yours. Jesus is offering you the benefits of his death – the forgiveness he won as he died in your place for your sins. You only need to ask Jesus for mercy, and he'll give it to you, welcoming you into God's family and transforming you into a child of God.

So, do not transpose your own self-condemnation onto the face of God. There is a place to weep over your sin, because it was your sin that sent Jesus to the cross. But always remember that Jesus went willingly, he went because he loves you, and he went not to reject you but to provide a way for you to be in the love of your heavenly Father.

If you have been convicted of your sin, and you've put your trust in Jesus, perhaps the challenge for you now is to see yourself as God sees you. Not as a terrible sinner, but a loved, forgiven, righteous child of God. For Peter, for you, and for me, shame is not the end of our story.

The messenger

This is where we will leave Jesus for little while. It seems odd, in the retelling of these stories throughout this book, to leave Jesus right at the climax, just as he is in the moment of greatest peril. But as we're telling the stories of the disciples, and they abandoned

Jesus, we'll have to pick up the story later on.[53] But to refresh your memory, here's a quick summary of what happened next, like one of those recaps you can watch on YouTube before the next season of your favourite show comes out: Jesus was all alone in his arrest, his torture, his public humiliation as the crowds called for his death, and his eventual execution on a cross. It was only at the foot of the cross, as Jesus hung there naked, with nails through his hands and feet, that we know Jesus had company – his mother and a few other women, and the disciple John. But even there, Jesus was to experience his greatest pain as he was forsaken by his Father. Eventually, at around three in the afternoon on the day after his arrest in the garden, Jesus died. He was buried in a tomb and a stone was rolled over the entrance to be eventually forgotten by history.

Normally that would be the end of the story.

But this isn't any normal story.

On the third day after Jesus' death, some of his female disciples – Mary Magdalene and Salome – and his mother went to his tomb to anoint his body. Yet when they got there, they found the stone had been rolled away and Jesus' body was missing. Instead, there was an angel there who had a message for them: '"Don't be alarmed," he said. "You are looking for Jesus the Nazarene, who was crucified. He has risen! He is not here. See the place where they laid him. But go, tell

---

53. If you do not know the story of what happened after Jesus' arrest and trial, then you really should read it. You can find it in the final chapters of the books of Matthew, Mark, Luke, and John.

his disciples and Peter, 'He is going ahead of you into Galilee. There you will see him, just as he told you'"' (Mark 16:6–7).

Jesus had risen from the dead, just as he had said he would, and he had gone to Galilee. Jesus was entrusting the message of his resurrection to these faithful women. The angel asked them to give the message particularly to Peter. Peter may have screwed up, but Jesus wasn't done with him – not by a long shot.

And no matter who you are or what you've done, Jesus isn't done with you either – not by a long shot.

14

THOMAS WHO ONCE DOUBTED

Jesus Appears to Thomas
John 20:24-29

I have a problem with New Year's Eve. It always promises to be the best night of the year, except it never is. When I was a teenager and in my early 20s, I had very high expectations. Every year I would go to a spot overlooking Sydney Harbour and watch the fireworks with friends. Apart from catching the train home packed in with thousands of drunk people, it was usually a pretty good night – but never the best night of the year.

As I got a bit older, I decided to try the low-key New Year's Eve. One year, I spent the night at a friend's house by the beach. We played games, chatted, ate good food, and slept in the next morning. That was a pretty amazing New Year's, so the next year I decided to replicate it.

So when my friends and family invited me to go to a spot next to the harbour to watch the fireworks, I politely declined – I was done with that. I had discovered the quiet life. I decided to stay home with my housemates who were having some friends over. But the fun, relaxed night didn't quite eventuate the way I had hoped. Most people had gone home or to bed by 10:30pm. At midnight, one housemate was doing the washing up and I was lying on the couch playing games on my phone.

About half an hour into the new year, I received a phone call from my sister, who was very excited to talk to me. She had just got engaged. Her boyfriend had taken her down to a secluded spot next to the water just after midnight and proposed. She said 'Yes!', they dropped the ring, lost it in the dark, found it again, and then returned to the group to share the good news. Many of my friends and family were there to celebrate with them. They hugged, kissed, and drank champagne (I assume). And where was I? I was on the couch playing games, missing one of the most significant moments of my family's life.

This poor Thomas missed out and so did Thomas, the disciple of Jesus.

After the women discovered Jesus' empty tomb, and the male disciples confirmed that the tomb was indeed empty, Jesus appeared first to Mary Magdalene, and then to his disciples.[54] We read in John 20 that the disciples

---

54. It seems like a particularly male thing to do, to have to check that the women hadn't made a mistake when they said that Jesus'

were all gathered together in a locked room, afraid that the people who had killed Jesus were going to come for them next, when Jesus appeared among them. He said, 'Peace be with you!' (v. 19), which was their standard greeting of *Shalom*. It's like saying 'Hey there!' but with more spiritual goodwill. But if we take this greeting literally, it was the perfect thing to say, because I assume that if a guy you thought was dead suddenly appeared among you, you wouldn't have peace. You'd scream like I scream when I find a spider in my car. I was thinking about what I would have said if I were Jesus, and I would either go with 'Surprise!', 'Ta–da!', or 'Peter, you still owe me three bucks.' I guess this is just one more reason why it's best that I'm not the Messiah and Jesus is.

During his visit, Jesus blessed the disciples and commissioned them for service to him before leaving again. We're not told if he disappeared or just used the door like an unresurrected person. After Jesus left, Thomas arrived: 'Now Thomas (also known as Didymus), one of the Twelve, was not with the disciples when Jesus

---

body was missing and that he had risen. As if perhaps they may have just found the wrong empty tomb because only men have a superior ability to tell one tomb from another. Or perhaps they wanted to make sure the women hadn't just looked in the wrong part of the tomb. Although to be fair, if someone tells you that the body of someone you love is missing, you're going to go check, no matter who it is. Still, it gives me great pleasure that the first person to meet the resurrected Jesus was Mary Magdalene (John 20:11–18). While, at first, she mistakes Jesus for a gardener (was he pushing a wheelbarrow?), the moment she recognises him is because he says her name. This, to me, is one of the most beautiful moments in Scripture.

came. So the other disciples told him, "We have seen the Lord!" But he said to them, "Unless I see the nail marks in his hands and put my finger where the nails were, and put my hand into his side, I will not believe"' (John 20:24–25).

There are a lot of interesting things in these two verses. First, there is relief that my parents called me Thomas and not Didymus. Second, I wonder where Thomas was while Jesus was visiting the other disciples. Why wasn't Thomas with them? Was he too depressed to join them? Had he slept in that morning? Had he just stepped out to get himself a kebab, and then walked in holding his lamb-with-the-lot and said, 'What did I miss?' The mystery of the missing Thomas is one that will stay with me until the day I die.

Third, of all the things to miss out on, missing out on being there when the resurrected Jesus visited his disciples for the first time is a pretty big thing to miss. A lot bigger than missing your sister's engagement.

Finally, I think Thomas' incredulity that Jesus had risen from the dead makes total sense. Thomas has gotten a bad rap for demanding to see Jesus' wounds before he believes that he rose from the dead, so much so that he has been given the name 'Doubting Thomas'. I think this is really unfair. He only doubted once; it's not like he spent his whole life doubting. A much more reasonable name for him would be Thomas Who Once Doubted.

What's more, if you're going to doubt anything, doubting that a guy who was executed on a cross and stabbed through the side is back from the dead is a pretty legitimate thing to doubt. There are some things that we shouldn't really spend a lot of time doubting – like whether the earth is round, whether vaccines work, and whether *Die Hard* is the greatest action movie of all time. But people coming back from the dead is not the kind of thing one should just unquestioningly accept. I know that Jesus did say on multiple occasions that he was going to rise again, but it's not as if any of the disciples figured out what he meant. Thomas was no less believing than the others; he just wasn't in the room where it happened.

We're told that no one saw Jesus again for a whole week. What Jesus was doing during that week, I have no idea. The Bible doesn't tell us. I like to believe that Jesus went on a holiday. I have zero evidence for that, but he certainly deserved a holiday: he had just saved the world. After his resurrection he had his snazzy resurrection body that could just appear and disappear at will. Wouldn't it make sense to appear in some secluded tropical paradise and just read, nap, fish, and eat coconuts for a few days? Or perhaps go and see all the things he created, from a human perspective? To visit Uluru, the Grand Canyon, or Iguazu Falls, that'd be fun. Like I said, there is no evidence that Jesus did any of these things, but there's no evidence that he didn't either.

Whatever Jesus did during that week, I feel like Thomas must have been having a terrible time. All the other disciples would have been over the moon that their beloved teacher and Lord was back, and Thomas was left out. He may have wanted to believe that Jesus was alive, but how could he? It must have been the loneliest week of his life.

But a week after his first appearance, Jesus turned up again, and this time Thomas was there. The doors were locked again, but Jesus had no time for doors anymore and turned up among them, saying once again, 'Peace be with you'[55] (John 20:26). Then Jesus turned to Thomas and said, 'Put your finger here; see my hands. Reach out your hand and put it into my side. Stop doubting and believe' (v. 27). How did Jesus know what Thomas had said? He wasn't there when Thomas said it. I assume he didn't have spies in the room, and he wasn't listening under the window. It was probably just one of those times when Jesus just *knew*. He had a knack for that.

We're not told if Thomas actually did put his finger in the nail marks, or his hand in Jesus side, but I suspect he didn't. It might have seemed like a good idea a week ago, but now Jesus was standing in front of him, he probably realised it'd be really rude – like if you were to reach out and rub the place where someone had had their limb amputated. It wouldn't be the done thing.

What Thomas did do, however, is extraordinary. He said to Jesus, 'My Lord and my God!' (v. 28). Thomas recognised what it meant that Jesus was back from the dead: he wasn't just an extraordinary man; he is God himself. Thomas is the person in John's Gospel to finally,

---

55. To which all the Anglicans in the room replied, 'And also with you.'

truly understand who Jesus is. Thomas went from being the loudest doubter to the most confident believer.

After Thomas' confession, Jesus said to him, 'Because you have seen me, you have believed; blessed are those who have not seen and yet have believed' (v. 29). The disciples were given a great gift in getting to see the risen Jesus. But for the vast majority of Christians across history, they wouldn't receive the same gift as Thomas and the others. We don't get to physically meet the risen Jesus – at least not till we die or he returns. Yet, we are blessed to believe in the risen Jesus on the strength of the eyewitness accounts of the disciples and the way we 'see' him at work in our lives.

Asking questions

What I love about this story is Jesus' response to Thomas' doubt. Doubt is not an uncommon experience for the follower of Jesus. It's easy to go through the Christian life believing that we should never question anything we're taught, or anything that we read in the Bible. We feel bad if we aren't always sure if God is real or if Jesus really is who the Bible says he is. We feel like we should have strong, unwavering faith always. But when we see how Jesus responded to Thomas, we see that Jesus responds to doubt not with condemnation but kindness.

Jesus had told the disciples that he would die and be raised to life. So when Thomas didn't believe that he was back, he could easily have blasted him when he turned up that second time:

'Here I am, Thomas! Is this good enough for you? Huh? I said I'd rise from dead, and you didn't believe me? Why did I even bother talking if you weren't going to listen to me? You're going to need to be made of stronger stuff than this if you're going to make it as an apostle, Tommy. Get your act together, mate!'

But when Jesus met Thomas, he wasn't angry or offended by his doubt. He was gentle and offered him the evidence he asked for – no matter how inappropriate the request was.

One of the problems facing Christians today is that often we don't feel that we're allowed to doubt. To express, or even acknowledge, that we're unsure about some basic tenet of our faith can feel like a terrible sin. And too often when we express our doubts, we are given pat answers, or people freak out that we might be losing our faith. When we notice questions rise within us, we try to clamp down on them, just in case the answers take us to a place where we don't want to go. To question the basic beliefs that make up our faith can feel like a betrayal of God and all the people who love us and taught us about him.

When I was in my early twenties, I was working as a youth minister at a church. One night I found myself on a website for ex-Christians, where people posted their stories of how they lost their faith, and why they had come to that place. I remember reading about all these doubts that people had and wondering if they were valid. I started to feel uncomfortable and stopped reading, just in case I got enticed into not being a Christian.

However, for weeks, my mind kept coming back to those stories. I could feel the doubts piling up, like mess threatening to tumble out of an overfull closet. What if I was making a mistake? What if there really wasn't a God? What if everything those people had said was true? I wasn't quite sure what I would do. I was on staff at a church, so I wasn't in a great position to question my faith.

I remember feeling anxious and depressed, till one night I had had enough. I sat down and wrote a prayer to a God I wasn't 100 per cent sure was there. I told him that I was going to seek truth, because if God was real then the truth couldn't hurt him, and if he wasn't real then I didn't want to believe a lie. Having done this, I went back to the website and read, and read, and read. I found then that when I allowed myself to face up to the doubts, they lost their power. They weren't forbidden questions that I wasn't allowed to ask; they were just queries that I should look into. Did I have all the answers to their doubts? No. But I also didn't feel like I had to, at least not right then. For the moment, I would keep doing the acts of faith, I would keep praying to God (who may or may not exist), I would keep reading my Bible, and I would keep meeting with his people. I decided that until I discovered that God wasn't real, I would live as if he was.

I remember waking up one morning while on holiday, in Adelaide of all places, and I believed again. I hadn't done anything to change things, but I knew things had changed. God had restored my faith in him.

It felt like those mornings when you wake up to a day of sunshine after weeks of rain. Once again I was sure that God was there and that he loved me.

Since then, I can't say that all my doubts are gone. Now, I have some answers to the issues those ex-Christians had, but I also have new questions. Over time, I might find more answers to some of those questions, and I know I'll find more questions. I can't say that I am always 100 per cent sure that Christianity is true. But when I have doubts, I am reminded of a story of when a lot of Jesus' followers left him. Jesus asked Peter and the other eleven disciples if they also wanted to leave Jesus, to which Peter's responded, 'To whom shall we go? You have the words of eternal life' (John 6:68). Sometimes I am totally in love with Jesus, and sometimes he's the only option I have. What holds me close to Jesus in the end is not my intellectual satisfaction (though I am often intellectually satisfied), but my relationship with Jesus. Without my relationship, my faith would be merely facts, which will not always satisfy me in the face of overwhelming doubt.

I'm telling you this story because I don't want you to be afraid of doubt, and I don't want to you be scared of asking questions. I have spent a lot more time since those days talking to people about why they lost their faith and reading stories about people who have stopped following Jesus. Sometimes, the big problem is that people felt like they weren't allowed to question their faith. Either they received a bad response from leaders when they did ask, or they had the impression that they couldn't even raise the subject. When they did ask the question, it carried the weight of betraying everything they ever held to be true, rather than merely asking a question to which they would like to find an answer. So let me tell you right now, you can ask questions, and you should ask questions. Unasked questions will grow like a cancer in your heart. Asked questions can exercise your faith, making it stronger and more robust.

Let me give you a non-exhaustive list of the questions you're allowed to raise:

Is God real?
Is God good?
Did Jesus exist?
Did Jesus rise from the dead?
Was the world created in six days?
Is the big bang real?
Are other religions valid?
Is sex outside marriage a sin?
Is same-sex marriage okay?
Is the Bible the word of God?
Are there mistakes in the Bible?
Does hell exist?
Can a God of love really send people to hell?

Ask your questions. And if people get offended, remember Jesus' gentle response to Thomas: his kindness to show him his hands and side. Jesus won't condemn you for your questions, so don't let others condemn you either.

Getting answers

Asking questions is all well and good. However, asking questions is only doing half the job. Notice that Jesus didn't avoid Thomas and leave him in his doubts; he called Thomas to move beyond his doubts: 'Stop doubting and believe.' Jesus was happy to meet Thomas' in his doubt, but he wasn't happy to leave him in his questions. There is a time when Jesus calls us to let go of the questions and throw our lot in with faith.

Thomas got the answers he was looking for, but that doesn't mean that we always will. As Jesus said to Thomas, 'Because you have seen me, you have believed; blessed are those who have not seen and yet have believed.' We do not have the same access to Jesus that his disciples did, but we are still called to faith in Jesus. This means we're not always going to get satisfactory answers to the questions we have, and we're not always going to be comfortable with every aspect of our faith. But there is blessing for us when we choose to believe, despite the fact that we can't verify everything we want to know with 100 per cent certainty.

'Faith is the flesh that grows on the skeleton of doubt.' This is a misquote from the writer Philip Yancey that I have drawn comfort from.[56] I read it (or didn't read it, as the facts may be) in his book *Reaching for the*

---

56. The real quote is: 'Doubt is the skeleton in the closet of faith, and I know no better way to treat a skeleton than to bring it into the open and expose it for what it is: not something to hide or fear, but a hard structure on which living tissue may grow.' Certainly more eloquent than my misquote, but at least mine is shorter. P. Yancey, *Reaching for the Invisible God* (Grand Rapids: Zondervan, 2000) 41.

Invisible God where he writes on doubt. He talks about how there can be no faith without doubt. If there was no doubt, then there wouldn't be faith, just certainty. Doubt must exist for faith to grow.[57]

As we face up to our questions, we need to accept that they are always going to be a companion to our faith. Doubt does not need to be a threat, but a sometimes uncomfortable friend who calls us down quiet and difficult paths that lead us to discover more of who God is. Unsure about the resurrection? Don't throw in the towel; investigate the evidence there is for it. Feeling burned by the sin of Christians? Don't write off Christianity, but look at the life of Jesus and see what you can learn from a man who was killed by the religious elites. Unsure if the Bible is trustworthy? Then investigate whether the Bible can be trusted. I suspect if you ask those questions, your faith will only

---

57. 'But what about Hebrews 11:1?' I hear you asking. The old NIV translation of Hebrews 11:1 says this: 'Now faith is being sure of what we hope for and certain of what we do not see' (NIV 1984). Being 'sure' and 'certain' doesn't leave a lot of room for doubt, does it?

The current translation is probably a little more helpful in that regard: 'Now faith is confidence in what we hope for and assurance about what we do not see' (NIV 2011). It is important to remember not to take this verse out of context. Hebrews 11:1 is the beginning of a long list of people who did impressive things because of their faith in God. Go read it – it's a great chapter. The verse isn't an overarching definition of faith, but a picture of faith that leads people to act in extraordinary ways in the face of incredible odds. When you choose to act in faith because of your confidence and assurance in the character of God, you're choosing, despite your doubts, to act in the way he is calling you to even if it costs you. Doubt can co-exist with faith, but faith requires us to act out of our belief that the God we meet in Jesus is alive, real, and who he says he is.

become stronger. You'll gain greater certainty about the resurrection, a faith that's more closely aligned to Jesus rather than the obedience of his followers, and a deeper appreciation of the strength of the Bible.

When I talk about Jesus with people who aren't Christians, sometimes they'll throw their questions at me, not really to find answers, but just as an exercise to illustrate the absurdity of my faith. These are not really questions worth asking, because they aren't looking for answers, and the asker isn't willing to change if they find a satisfactory answer. But there are other times when people will ask me the same questions and they genuinely want to know the answer. If your questions are asked so that you might genuinely discover the truth about God, Jesus, life, and faith, then prayerfully keep asking them, trusting that the Holy Spirit will lead into truth, and see where they take you.

There is a time to stop doubting and believe, but I think there is also a time to keep doubting as you keep believing. It says in Matthew 7, 'Ask and it will be given to you; seek and you will find; knock and the door will be opened to you. For everyone who asks receives; the one who seeks finds; and to the one who knocks, the door will be opened' (vv. 7–8).

It was Thomas' doubt that led him to meet the risen Christ and confess him as 'Lord and God'. Ask your questions, seek your answers, and you too will find the risen Christ.

15

'PETER, DO YOU LOVE ME?'

Jesus Meets the Disciples by the Lake
John 21:1-19

There's something magical about seeing friends unexpectedly.

One time, one of my best friends (we'll call him Ryan because that's his name) had been overseas in South and Central America for months.[58] We hadn't expected him to come home for a few more months, but he booked a trip back to Australia and didn't tell anyone. When he arrived at Sydney Airport there was no one there to pick him up, because no one knew he was coming. In one final act of embracing the poor backpacker culture, he

_____
58. This is the same Ryan with the long golden hair from Chapter 13.

decided to walk home. His house was over 40km from the airport, but Ryan didn't let that stop him. He wandered home and finally arrived around midnight.[59] The next day, when I heard that he was home, I was so excited, and I went over to see him as soon as I could. I loved getting to spend time with my old friend again.

Then there was the time when another of my best friends (we'll call him David because that is his name) had been in India for half a year doing aid work.[60] He snuck home early to come to a weekly dinner with my friends. It was fantastic to see him. When another friend was about to arrive at the dinner, we told David to go hide, so he could pop out when she came into the room and surprise her like a friendly returned traveller poltergeist. He hid, and when she turned up, he jumped out from around the corner, slipped on a mat, and fell over – hitting his chin on a step on the way down. He started bleeding on himself and the tiled floor. His entrance was very surprising indeed! I felt very honoured to be the one who took our returned, injured hero to the medical centre to get stitches in his chin.

---

59. As an interesting aside, I'm pretty sure on that trip overseas Ryan was on a bus that got caught in the middle of a firefight between police and drug cartels. He's led a much more interesting life than me. Although, I did once see a car drive up the back of another car at the traffic lights, so don't think I haven't seen some of my own crazy stuff.

60. Here's another piece of trivia: David's name in my phone is not David, it's Linda Hotty. I put it in there when I was single so that when he messaged or called me I could show people and say 'Oh, I'm just getting messages from attractive women.' I sure did look impressive.

I think I can say that Jesus' return from the dead was at least 100 per cent more astonishing than any surprise return of my friends, even though Jesus had very clearly told the disciples it was going to happen. So it stands to reason that having Jesus around took a lot longer to feel real than it took for it to feel normal to have Ryan and David home earlier than expected.

The returned Jesus was a bit of a flighty chap. After he rose from the dead, he wasn't constantly with the disciples. Where he was is a significant question. I did suggest in the last chapter that he may have gone on sightseeing trips around the world. I have a friend who suggested to me that Jesus was popping back and forth between heaven and earth with his new dimension-travelling body, but I think there is about as much evidence for that as for my beach holiday idea. It's all a mystery, sadly. All we know is the recorded appearances that have been given to us in the Bible, and after Jesus appeared to Thomas and the other ten disciples, it took a little while for Jesus to turn up again.

When he did turn up, it was in Galilee. In Mark 16:7 the angels told the women at the tomb, 'He is going ahead of you into Galilee. There you will see him, just as he told you.' Well, in John 21 we learn that seven of the disciples, Peter, James, John, Thomas, Nathanael, and two others, headed back to Galilee – presumably because that's where Jesus had told them to go.

While they were there, Peter let everyone know that he was going fishing, and the others decided that sounded grand so they went with him. This rekindled enthusiasm for fishing was most likely because they had nothing better to do. Things would have been a little unclear for the disciples at that point in time. They had seen Jesus twice, briefly both times, when he appeared among them, but that was it. Now that Jesus was alive but hadn't given them any instructions, what were they meant to do? It's like when you go to the doctor, you're sitting in the waiting room and your doctor comes out, and they say, 'I'll be with you in a sec.' And then they go back into their consulting room, not to come out for half an hour. What are you meant to do while you sit there waiting? Have they forgotten about you? Are they actually going to come back? Did they leave via the back door because you're gross and they really don't want to have to deal with you and your hypochondria again? This waiting period is stressful. So, you pretend to read a gossip magazine from 1992 and hope your doctor hasn't just ghosted you, because you don't know if your self-esteem can cope with that again. That might be something of how the disciples were feeling.

But more significantly, how must Peter have been feeling? Were things between him and Jesus awkward? It wouldn't surprise me if Peter went fishing to get his mind off all the craziness that had been going on. Fishing, much like reading a magazine in the doctor's surgery, was a concrete activity that was much less confusing than trying to figure out what it meant that Jesus was alive but had only bothered to visit you twice.

Sadly, the disciples didn't have a good night fishing. In the morning, there was a guy standing on the shore, and he called out to them, 'Friends, haven't you any fish?' (John 21:5).

They replied that they hadn't, so the guy on the shore suggested they throw their nets on the other side of the boat. As soon as they did, the net filled up with fish.

Realising that they'd seen this trick before when Jesus had first called them to follow him, John turned to Peter and said, 'It is the Lord!' (v. 7).

Peter, impulsive as ever, grabbed his coat, threw it on, dived in the water, and started swimming towards Jesus! I love that Peter gets dressed to go swimming. The original Greek literally says that Peter was naked in the boat. It can mean that either he (along with the other fishing disciples) was actually starkers, or that he was just wearing a loin cloth, the ancient equivalent of fishing in his tighty-whities. I'll let you pick whichever option you prefer, but however he was dressed for fishing, he definitely overdressed for swimming. (The nudity of the disciples may have accounted for why they didn't catch any fish. If I were swimming around in those waters, I would stay well away from a boat full of nude dudes.)

I also like the fact that Peter was so impatient to get to Jesus that he jumped overboard and swam. Why would that be faster than taking the boat? I like to think that as Peter was swimming into shore, the other disciples sailed past him yelling, 'We'll see you there!' However, Peter did actually make the right call because the Bible says the other disciped 'followed' in the boat. I guess the huge haul of future fish fingers must have slowed the boat down significantly, but that amuses me less, so I'll just hold the image of Peter being overtaken by the fishing boat in my mind as a little bit of alternative Bible history.

When they arrived, Jesus was cooking some food: a little bread and a little fish. He asked them to bring him some of the fish they caught. Peter, being a bit of a rig, dragged the net full of 153 fish ashore. Jesus then invited his mates to have breakfast with him. I love the idea of Jesus cooking breakfast for his disciples. He's risen from the dead, and he's still serving them. He is giving them their daily bread. It also makes me wonder how good Jesus' cooking was. If I get to the new creation and Jesus invites me around for a barbecue, I am definitely going to be there – partly for the free food and partly to satisfy my curiosity about Jesus' culinary skills.

As they were gathered around the fire, there was still some weird tension in the air. John puts it like this: 'None of the disciples dared ask him, "Who are you?" They knew it was the Lord' (v. 12).

Why would they want to ask Jesus who he was if they knew it was him? Maybe Jesus' resurrection body made him look different enough that he would sometimes not be recognised, but the same enough that there was no doubt it was him, despite what their eyes were seeing.

At some point, probably after the meal, Jesus turned to Peter and had this conversation with him:

'Simon son of John, do you love me more than these?'

'Yes, Lord,' he said, 'you know that I love you.'

Jesus said, 'Feed my lambs.'

Again Jesus said, 'Simon son of John, do you love me?'

He answered, 'Yes, Lord, you know that I love you.'

Jesus said, 'Take care of my sheep.'

The third time he said to him, 'Simon son of John, do you love me?'

Peter was hurt because Jesus asked him the third time, 'Do you love me?' He said, 'Lord, you know all things; you know that I love you.'

Jesus said, 'Feed my sheep.' (vv. 15–17)

After Peter's public assurance at the Last Supper that he would not deny Jesus, and his public denials of his Lord at the house of the high priest, Jesus was giving him a public redemption. Three times Peter denied Jesus; three times Jesus asked Peter to reaffirm his love.

What must it have meant to Peter to have had this interaction? Had Peter been weighed down by uncertainty about his relationship with Jesus? Was he expecting a public rebuke from his master? Jesus doesn't shy away from Peter's failing, but he doesn't publicly scold him either. Instead, Jesus restores him and commissions him for service. Remember Jesus' prayer for Peter before he denied him? 'Simon, Simon, Satan has asked to sift all of you as wheat. But I have prayed for you, Simon, that your faith may not fail. And when you have turned back, strengthen your brothers' (Luke 22:31–32). This was Jesus following through on that prayer. Peter had turned back, and now Jesus was calling him to strengthen his brothers as he leads this new movement of Jesus followers.

What does this tell us about the kind of leaders Jesus is looking for? He obviously isn't looking for perfect leaders. He's looking for those who, after failing, turn back to Jesus and use their restoration to strengthen those they are called to lead.

For Peter, denying Jesus was his darkest moment, the time when he saw himself most clearly. All his bravado was stripped away, and he was confronted with the true nature of his heart. Had Jesus not had this conversation with him, I can imagine Peter would have been forever a broken man, defined by his sin. But Jesus was giving Peter a new story. He wasn't erasing his past or minimising his sin. Jesus was restoring him and using the moment of Peter's greatest weakness to become the place from which he would rebuild his character. In asking Peter to feed his sheep, Jesus was calling him to his role of leadership in the new church. It was because of Peter's fall and restoration that he was truly ready to be the leader he was called to be. Jesus wanted Peter to be a leader who knew himself. He wanted Peter to be a leader who wasn't under any illusions about his own abilities, but defined by his relationship to Jesus.

Can you imagine putting the guy who publicly rebuked Jesus, or chopped off a guy's ear, in charge of a church, let alone a new movement that would one day become the largest religion in history? That would seem to be a terrible idea. But the leader who knows the extent of their own weakness, who is defined by a fundamental mistrust of themselves and a total trust in Jesus, is exactly the kind of leader who can change the world. That was the leader Jesus called that day by the beach.

No doubt, you can look at your own moments of greatest sin, the times when the true depth of your depravity has been laid bare, so you cannot lie to yourself about your inherent goodness anymore. Even if no one else has seen it, Jesus has. When you think of these times, do you despair?

How is your relationship with Jesus in light of your sin? Are you awkward around him? Do you feel like he's not all that happy with you? Or that he's just putting up with you because he has to? Remember, just like when Jesus looked at Peter when he denied him, Jesus isn't looking at you with condemnation.

Read the conversation between Jesus and Peter again, but this time, imagine you are sitting by that fire with Jesus. The disciples are sitting around, and Jesus asks you if you love him. How do you respond? Go on, try it.

If you love Jesus, and I assume you do, then you will respond just like Peter. You will tell Jesus that of course you love him. As Jesus presses you, you may feel hurt, like Peter, that Jesus is questioning your commitment, but you may also find the weight of your guilt being lifted off you as you realise that Jesus is calling you, once again, to follow him.

What does Jesus call you to? Perhaps he isn't calling you to become the leader of the church, or even a church, or even a leader at all. But I can guarantee you one thing: he is calling you. He is restoring you and calling you to follow him so that you might serve him by playing your part in bringing his kingdom to earth.

You don't have to be defined by your sin. If you've come to Jesus in repentance, he has restored you. He has forgiven your sin, but he hasn't erased your past. The things you have done, and been forgiven for, are now part of your story moving forward. Your life will be a trophy of God's grace. The fruit of your obedience is a testament to the goodness of God to take what is broken and make it new – to take what was dead and bring it to life.

Don't listen to the lie that your sin disqualifies you from serving Jesus. Bring it to him, confess it, and let it become part of your story as you follow him closer every day.

How you're going to die

The final time that Jesus asked Peter to feed his sheep, he continued on to tell Peter how he was going to die: 'Jesus said, "Feed my sheep. Very truly I tell you, when you were younger you dressed yourself and went where you wanted; but when you are old you will stretch out your hands, and someone else will dress you and lead you where you do not want to go." Jesus said this to indicate the kind of death by which Peter would glorify God. Then he said to him, "Follow me!"' (John 21:17b–19).

If you could hear how you were going to die, would you want to know? Jesus obviously thought it was important that Peter knew, and so he described, in vague terms, Peter's future demise. Many people interpret the stretching out of hands as Jesus describing Peter's death by crucifixion, which is the traditional view of how he died.

I think knowing how I was going to die would just make me feel sick with anticipation of the pain. My wife likes to squeeze blackheads out of my face, and even waiting for that pain hurts. So waiting for years on end in anticipation that at some point I would be experiencing crucifixion would probably be excruciating.

So why would Jesus tell Peter? Because Peter promised that he would die for Jesus. In John 13:37, before Jesus predicted Peter's denial, he promised his Lord, 'I will lay down my life for you.' But that very night Peter denied him.

Jesus' prediction of Peter's death is part of his restoration. Jesus didn't tell him just to show off his fortune-telling skills, to make Peter depressed, or to warn Peter so he could avoid his death (like characters are tempted to do in at least fifty per cent of all time-travel movies). He wanted Peter to know that he wouldn't let Jesus down again. He was giving him confidence that he would be able to live up to his own ideals.

So perhaps the question is not, 'Would you like to know how you're going to die?' but, 'Would you like to know that you're going to live up to Jesus' call?' That I would like to know. It would give me so much confidence to know that I was not going to let Jesus down in the future like I have in the past.

Do you ever worry that you're letting Jesus down? The truth is, while you will sin again, in the long run, you're not going to let Jesus down. If you are a Christian, you can be 'confident of this, that he who began a good work in you will carry it on to completion until the day of Christ Jesus' (Philippians 1:6). Jesus has taken responsibility to make you into the person he wants you to be. That doesn't mean that you're not responsible for the choices you make; it just means Jesus has a lot invested in helping you be conformed to his image. He will play his part in transforming you to be the person he has created you to be.

So as you face up to your sin, face up to Jesus' love and forgiveness. If he's not dwelling on it, you don't need to either. You may think that his disappointment with you means he'd prefer to use someone else, someone more qualified. But remember, you can't disappoint Jesus. He knows you better than you know yourself. And he knew it all before he called you to himself. You may be tempted to withdraw and leave the Jesus following for those who are more cut out for it. But just as Jesus called Peter to follow him again, he's calling you to do it too. It's time to go where Jesus is calling you.

16

JESUS SKIPS TOWN

Jesus' Commission and Ascension
Acts 1:1-11

I go on a lot of camps. When I say camps, I'm not talking
about sleeping-in-tents camps, but camps where you stay
in cabins, play large group games, have mealtimes in a
big hall, listen to Bible talks in the mornings, and you
have a big campfire on the last night where everyone
talks about what a great time they've had and how
they're going to miss everyone.

The reason why I go on these camps is not because
I'm pretending to be a teenager and signing up for a
week of exciting outdoor activities with other 'kids my
age', because that would be weird (to put it mildly). I am
often on these camps as the speaker. This means it's my
job to give the Bible talks each day.

What I have noticed about these camps, especially
the ones that go for a whole week, is that there is a

familiar rhythm to them. When everyone arrives, there's a lot of awkwardness. Some people have come alone and don't know anyone. Some people have a few friends. And some are the regulars who come every year and know lots of campers and leaders. The first day or two, people are getting to know each other, friendship cliques are forming, cabin groups become good friends, and romances might be kindling.

By the middle of camp, almost everyone is having a good time. People who knew no one have made friends; people who knew a few people know a lot more people. Some of the kids we thought were quiet have turned out to be not so quiet, while others have let on that they have some secret skill like juggling, beatboxing, or sneaking off with their new-found love.

Then come the last days of camp. Announcements get made like, 'This will be our last dinner together before we go home.' To which everyone responds dutifully with an 'Awww' or a 'Nooooo'. All the lasts are marked in this way: last meals, last activity times, last Bible talk, last bedtime, last lights out, no seriously this is your last lights out, please, everyone is tired and it's been a long camp just turn your lights out.

As the lasts are happening, many people are working at savouring the moment, remembering what it feels like to be there at that camp with those people. Usually there is a sharing time (often around the aforementioned campfire), and campers and leaders will talk about what they have loved about camp and the memories they'll cherish. A few people will cry. Sometimes almost everyone will cry.

On the final day, when the bags are all packed, the cabins have been deserted so the campsite cleaning staff can come through, and parents are arriving to pick up the campers, it's time for the last goodbyes. For some people, this means a lot of hugs and following each other on social media. For others, it's awkward because they don't know what to do. I'm always in the awkward category. As a leader, I'm not allowed to hug campers or follow them on social media, and there are always a few whose names I can't remember. If I say goodbye to someone, I have to say goodbye to everyone, and then I'll get to those people whose names I don't know – and they aren't wearing name tags anymore. I often just stand back and let people come to me. I'm not sure if that's the right thing to do, but who knows? Goodbyes are just difficult, no matter which way you cut it. The moment feels significant because the camp has been significant, especially for people who don't go on twenty camps a year,[61] but appropriately marking that significance is something I've never mastered.

So now, as we come to the end of Jesus' time on earth, I can imagine the final days with Jesus would be a whole lot more difficult than the end of a camp. I imagine for Jesus' disciples, their final days with him would have been like the final days of camp, but with the added weight of

---

61. As I write this, it's September 2020. I don't know when in the future you're reading this, but if 2020 means anything to you, you'll know that I've spent most of the year in lockdown at home avoiding the plague. So I only got to go on three camps this year before the world shut down and everything got cancelled. Who knows, maybe camps are a thing of the past and they'll never happen again, and this opening will mean nothing. I hope not. I like camps.

three years of living together and a death and resurrection to boot. Their last night campfire would have been a whopper! As they hung out with Jesus in those last days, they must have been overjoyed to have him back with them, but sad knowing that he would be leaving. How do you mark the end of an era like the era of the Messiah? Well, you can be sure that Jesus knew exactly what to do – and the disciples, as always, did not.

The highflyer

In Acts 1:3 we're told that Jesus appeared to the disciples 'over a period of forty days and spoke about the kingdom of God'. In those last days, Jesus kept turning up and giving the disciples his final instructions before he left earth. I imagine those were some of the most exciting times they spent with Jesus, and the least intense, just hanging out with their friend who was dead but alive again. Without the crowds pressing in, or the focused march towards Jerusalem, it probably had the feel of summer holidays. Except the problem was, he was always leaving – the time they had together was never going to last.

We're told in Matthew that when the time came for Jesus to leave them, the eleven disciples all headed up a mountain in Galilee and met Jesus there. It was a bit like when you go with your mate to the airport to see them off. We're told that 'When they saw him, they worshiped him; but some doubted' (Matthew 28:17). It seems pretty strange to me that some of them doubted. They were there with a dude who was dead and came back to life and had been popping in and out of locked rooms and making fish appear out of nowhere for the last six weeks, and still a few of them were like, 'I'm not sure this is legit.' Matthew never tells us which particular disciples were doubting, probably to protect their anonymity in heaven. At least Thomas came round when he met the resurrected Christ. These guys though. I guess they're the ancient equivalents of anti-vaxxers, flat earthers, and moon-landing deniers. And, well, isn't it nice to see that Jesus invites even them to follow him.

On the mountain, Jesus gave his disciples a job to do once he was gone: 'All authority in heaven and on earth has been given to me. Therefore go and make disciples of all nations, baptising them in the name of the Father and of the Son and of the Holy Spirit, and teaching them to obey everything I have commanded you. And surely I am with you always, to the very end of the age' (Matthew 28:18–20). Once Jesus left, he had no intention of the disciples all saying to each other, 'Well that was a wild few years!' then heading home, like the hobbits to the Shire at the end of *Return of the King*, to pick up where they left off like it was all some nice adventure that ended happily ever after. Jesus had a job for the disciples to do: bringing the good news of what he had done to all the nations. Jesus wanted them to change the world!

That's a little bit of a concerning thought. Considering all we have seen throughout this book, was that really a good idea? These were men who were thick, proud, argumentative, selfish, violent, intolerant, and cowardly. Not to mention those blokes who were currently doubting the resurrection in the presence of the resurrected Jesus! You would think that after three years with these guys, Jesus would have found some new people who were perhaps better suited to the task.

If we go back to Acts 1, we're told that Jesus was eating with his disciples and he said to them, 'Do not leave Jerusalem, but wait for the gift my Father promised, which you have heard me speak about. For John baptised with water, but in a few days you will be baptised with the Holy Spirit' (vv. 4–5).

The disciples, clearly not really listening to Jesus, asked him about something completely different: 'Lord, are you at this time going to restore the kingdom to Israel?' (v. 6). Jesus was telling them that they were about to get the Holy Spirit, and they were wondering if Jesus was finally, finally, going to take his place on the throne of the great King David and re-establish Israel as a world leader. This had been a live issue for the entirety of Jesus' ministry – he had just spent forty days teaching them about the kingdom of God – and they still thought Jesus was just going to be a very impressive political leader.

I don't know how many times you have to be told something for it to sink in, but I hope after three years, a death, and a resurrection, you'd be able to listen a little better than the disciples. Though to be fair, I've had two hands for at least thirty-eight years and I still don't always know the difference between my left and my right. And my wife's name is Emily, but the other night I called her Emma. We've only been together for seven years, so I can't be expected to have remembered her name yet, can I? Perhaps I'm not much sharper than the disciples.

How did Jesus respond to the disciples' question? He said, 'That's none of your business, now let me get back to the point I was making' (that's my paraphrase). He said to them: 'It is not for you to know the times or dates the Father has set by his own authority. But you will receive power when the Holy Spirit comes on you; and you will be my witnesses in Jerusalem, and in all Judea and Samaria, and to the ends of the earth' (vv. 7–8).

Just like in Matthew, Jesus gave them a job to do. They were to go into the world and be witnesses to what Jesus had done. They were to tell everyone that God had come to visit humanity, and he had lived, died, risen again, and was calling everyone to put their trust in him. Where were they to do this? In Jerusalem, in Judea and Samaria, and to the ends of the earth. Just as we talked about in Chapter 8, this isn't just a list of random places like 'London, Paris, Wakanda, and Bargo'. Jerusalem was a city, the centre of the Jewish faith. Judea was the region Jerusalem was in. Samaria was where the Samaritans lived, the mixed-race people who had some mixed-up form of Jewish faith. The ends of the earth were everywhere beyond that. Where I live in Melbourne is about as far from Jerusalem as you can get, so in terms of Jesus' command, I pretty much live at the end of the earth, and the gospel has even made it here. Jesus was commanding the disciples to the take the good news of who he was and what he had done, from the people most like them in faith and ethnicity to the people least like them. All people were to be welcomed into God's kingdom. This is the exact opposite of what the disciples were asking for – consolidating all the power in Jerusalem while Jesus rules on an earthly throne for his people. This is God's invitation to all people, through Jesus' disciples, in the power of the Holy Spirit: to join in what he has done for us in his Son.

With those inspiring last words, Jesus left: 'After he said this, he was taken up before their very eyes, and a cloud hid him from their sight' (v. 9).

I love this bit. Jesus said something cool then ascended into heaven! That guy is all class. Now in case you're concerned that Jesus just kept flying up, reached a speed of 11km per second, escaped earth's orbit, and roared off into space like some kind of ancient human deep-space probe, that's not what the Bible is implying. Of course Luke, who wrote this part of the Bible, had a different understanding of how space worked. For him, and all the people who lived in Jesus' day, heaven was up, so Jesus went up, to make it clear where he was going. At some point Jesus would have transitioned from our dimension to the dimension of the heavenly realms, a very real place but not a place we can physically access in our current state.

If Jesus had been on earth during our times, perhaps he would have faded out like he was in some kind of *Star Trek* transporter. For us, that might be dimension-changing visual language that we understand better than someone heading up into the sky like Superman. Whatever the case, Jesus didn't need to ascend into the sky to get to heaven (he arrived via Holy Spirit conception, so it's clear his method of dimension transport is flexible). He ascended as a sign to the watching disciples that his work was done, but he wasn't dying. He was leaving to go be at his Father's side. Verses 10–11 say, 'They were looking intently up into the sky as he was going, when suddenly two men dressed in white stood beside them. "Men of Galilee," they said, "why do you stand here looking into the sky? This same Jesus, who has been taken from you into heaven, will come back in the same way you have seen him go into heaven."'

I love the question the angels asked them, 'Why do you stand there looking into heaven?' Um, because a dude just flew into the clouds! Why wouldn't you be looking into the sky? If you see flying humans, the natural response is to look. Even if they've disappeared, you keep looking just in case they'll appear again – maybe on the other side of the cloud. I spend too much time looking at the opening of my apartment block's garbage chute, where it empties into the big bin, just in case I see someone's rubbish come flying into the skip – and that's just gravity doing its thing. I would definitely be looking for flying Jesus.

That said, the angels are making a statement with their question. They're saying, 'Stop wasting your time staring at the sky, Jesus has given you a job, it's time to get on with it.' So with that, the disciples headed back to Jerusalem, picked a replacement for Judas (a guy named Mathias, who got picked as an apostle and then was never mentioned again), and then settled in to wait for the promised Holy Spirit.

Why couldn't Jesus just hang around?

This brings me to a feeling that I often have. The Holy Spirit, as good as he is, seems like a bit of a letdown compared to Jesus. Don't get me wrong, I love the Holy Spirit, it's just I can't help thinking, wouldn't it have been wonderful if Jesus had just hung around? Jesus has a resurrection body that is never going to get sick or die, so he certainly could have chosen to stay on earth. Imagine being able to hang out with Jesus and ask him any question you want. You could sit down with him and actually chat to him, face to face, about your ethical dilemmas or romantic problems. How great would it be just to be able to rock up at Jesus' house anytime you want, to play Xbox or cook a great meal together? It would be amazing!

As nice as that sounds, there is a significant problem. We'd all love to spend time with Jesus, but it would be logistically difficult. As of right now, according to the googling I just did (yes, that's right, I am a scholar), there are about 2.3 billion Christians in the world. Assuming that all of them wanted to get some time with Jesus, and Jesus set up a system where he would spend five minutes with each person in groups of five, working eight hours a day, six days a week, it would take a really, really long time to get through them all. If he started on January 1 2022 he would finish on November 2 in the year 17,330, which, incidentally will be my 15,316th wedding anniversary.[62]

So when Jesus started telling his disciples that he was going to be leaving them and sending the Holy Spirit in his place, it may not have made sense to them, but on reflection it makes plenty of sense to us. The Holy Spirit can get a lot more done by dwelling within every Christian than Jesus ever could being physically confined to his body wherever he happened to be at any particular time.

Jesus promised the disciples before he died: 'I will ask the Father, and he will give you another advocate to help you and be with you forever – the Spirit of truth. The world cannot accept him, because it neither sees him nor knows him. But you know him, for he lives with you and will be in you' (John 14:16–17). Jesus wanted the disciples to know that he was leaving, but he wasn't leaving them alone to fend for themselves. In fact, Jesus made them this amazing promise: 'Very truly I tell you, whoever believes in me will do the works I have been doing, and they will do even greater things than these, because I am going to

---

62. I'm not that certain of that maths. I just did it with a spreadsheet, my calculator, and a page I found online. I didn't account for leap years, because that seems too difficult. I figure Jesus could have one extra day off a year every four years because he deserves it. Anyway, I could ask a proper mathematician to do the maths, but then Jesus' work might not end on my wedding anniversary and that would be disappointing. The main point is, it'd take Jesus a really, really long time.

the Father' (John 14:12). Imagine doing greater things than Jesus. How is that even possible? Jesus wasn't promising the disciples that the things they did would ever be greater than his death and resurrection – that great job was for Jesus and Jesus alone – but how many lives did Jesus change in his time on earth through a physical interaction? Thousands? Tens of thousands? That's significant! But remember there are 2.3 billion Christians on earth today. Jesus' followers have gone on to change the whole world! Billions of people have found hope and salvation in Jesus. People have found forgiveness, healing, and purpose in Jesus, because of the great acts of his followers empowered by the presence of the Holy Spirit.

And here's the really exciting news: we too are part of the 'greater things' that Jesus promised. If we are Christians, then the moment when we came to faith was part of the greater things that Jesus promised his disciples they would do. And as you obediently follow Jesus – as others come to faith because of your witness to the power of the resurrected Jesus in your life; when you pray for people and God changes their lives; if you get to see the Holy Spirit at work in the world around you – then you are part of doing the greater things that Jesus promised his disciples they would do. What a privilege!

'Ahh,' you might say. 'That all sounds great, but I am no spiritual giant. I'm a bumbler. I make mistakes. I sin way too often. I'm not very wise. I'm much more like the disciples we've read about than some hero of the faith who can do "greater things" and change the world.' I know. I feel the same way as you. Before I sat down to write today, I said to myself, 'I have to remember to pray before I do any writing.' But then I just wrote. I couldn't even manage to pray for a few minutes before I got down to typing, so why would I think I'm any kind of Christian leader? I get scared about talking to people about Jesus. I talk a lot more about caring for the poor than I actually care for people who are poor. I get bored during sermons at church, and I often don't feel anything when I sing worship songs. When I pray, I pray small prayers that are hard to quantify, because I'm scared of what will happen if God doesn't answer my prayers (even though I've seen God answer my prayers again and again). I have a job as a youth minister and I spend a lot of my time thinking I should be better at my job (even though I've been doing it a long time and I've seen God do great things through me). I don't expect God to speak to me, so when I do hear from him, I get surprised every time (even though I totally believe that God wants to communicate with us a lot more than we want to listen to him).

Okay, that's probably enough of the self-therapy for now. My point is, if you don't feel like you're anything special, I know how you feel. And you know what? I bet the disciples were feeling exactly the same way. Jesus had just given them the job of changing the whole world, and some of them still weren't sure if he was actually back from the dead. Which of them would have heard the angels challenging them to get on with the work Jesus had given them and thought, 'Right! Yep! No worries!'? Some of them may have been staring into the sky for a little longer than necessary just to put off the inevitable reckoning with the massive task that Jesus laid at their feet.

Jesus has gone into the sky, and one day he's coming back the way he came. But between now and then, he's given us a job to do. And if you feel as underqualified for the call of Jesus on your life as those disciples did on that hill in Galilee, then do not fear. It's the beginning of the greater things.

17

'WE ARE NOT DRUNK'

The Holy Spirit Arrives
Acts 2:1–41

Did I ever tell you about the time when I took on an intruder in my church in the middle of the night? No? Then let me tell you. I'm sure you'll think I'm a hero by the time I'm finished.

I used to work at a church where I was the youth minister, and in my spare time I was also part of a creative arts group that put on a show every year. The show would be full of video, dance, and drama. My job was often to look after all the video stuff. It was super fun to be a part of. We'd perform the show in the church and hundreds of people would come to watch. There would be lights and lasers, subwoofers and smoke machines. While for some churches that's just a normal Sunday, for us it was a huge production.

257

One year we'd done the show on a Saturday night, then arrived the next morning for church. I went up into the sound booth with another guy. After looking around the room he said to me, 'Tom, where's the computer? Where are the lights? Where are the lasers? Where are the amps? Where are the speakers? Where is the projector?'

As I followed where he was pointing, I could see he was right. Heaps of the stuff that had been in the church the night before was missing. Someone had come in and stolen thousands of dollars' worth of equipment.

Despite being the victims of a significant crime, we knew, as the old saying goes, 'The church-service-that-is-also-a-show must go on!' So we scrambled to get everything together, and we did it, but the next year we decided we didn't want to get robbed again. So after the Saturday night performance, the director of the show and I decided to sleep in the church. We were going to keep watch like the crime fighters we were. We set up our sleeping bags on the stage and went to sleep.

During the middle of the night, I woke up with a start. A door at the back of the church had been opened. I looked and saw a shadowy figure with a torch coming in through the back door.

Then I did the bravest thing I've ever done in my life. I jumped up out of my sleeping bag and walked straight at the man. I was wearing boxer shorts and a t-shirt. I suspect I looked very intimidating. My friend, the director, was right behind me.

I said, 'What are you doing?'

The man said, 'I'm security. What are you doing?'

I said, 'Oh *you're* security! *We're* security!'

I was ready to protect our lasers and smoke machines with my life. I knew kung fu.[63] I was ready to go.

But then I noticed the intruder was wearing a security guard's uniform. And our church did have security guards who came and checked on the church during their patrols. The guy I was trying to scare away was the guy whose job it was to protect the place that I was protecting.

As it turned out, we'd forgotten to lock the back door of the church. When the guard checked the doors, he found the door open, so he came in to make sure everything was okay. Lucky we figured that out before the director and I killed him with our bare hands. (If you've ever seen me in real life, you'd know that there is zero chance I could have killed him with my bare hands. I'm not really the kind of guy who could take on a security guard. There is a low chance I could take on anyone in a fight. If, in some odd piece of science fiction, I met an exact copy of myself and had to fight me, I'd still lose the fight.)[64]

---

63. Okay, I didn't know kung fu, but I had been to two classes once so I was pretty much an expert.

64. I'm pretty sure there was a film in the early 2000s where a bad Jet Li was travelling through multiple universes killing different versions of himself and absorbing their life power, till he had to fight the good Jet Li. There is no real point to this footnote, I just remembered the film as I was writing that sentence and thought I'd share my remembrance with you. I guess I could go look the film up on IMDB, but I've got a chapter to get back to.

The only reason I was able to confront the security guard at all was because I was filled with adrenalin and a great love for lasers and smoke machines. It's very surprising to me that I did anything other than cower in fear. I'm sure that pretty soon, the adrenalin would have run out and I would have just been a terrified, skinny white man, leaving the director to actually deal with the situation.

As we come to the end of our book, we have one last story to look at. And that's the story of what happened when Jesus' promise of the Holy Spirit came to pass. In this story the disciples, and particularly Peter, do something very surprising and much more impressive than what my director friend and I might have done that night in the church. And they didn't just do one surprising thing; they changed their whole lives.

Wind and fire

About a week after Jesus' ascension into heaven, the disciples and about 108 other followers of Jesus were hanging about in a house in Jerusalem. The Jewish festival of Pentecost (or the Feast of Weeks) was happening. This was a festival to celebrate the spring harvest, and was one that brought people to Jerusalem to celebrate. So as Jesus' followers gathered inside, praying and waiting for the Holy Spirit to come, outside, people from all over the known world gathered to celebrate Pentecost. Acts 2:2 says, 'Suddenly a sound like the blowing of a violent wind came from heaven and filled the whole house where they were sitting.'

Imagine that: you're in the middle of prayer, and the whole house begins to sound like you're in a cyclone, and yet, there's no actual wind. You would definitely think something was up. This wasn't subtle. Something very significant was going on.

Things just keep getting weirder: 'They saw what seemed to be tongues of fire that separated and came to rest on each of them. All of them were filled with the Holy Spirit and began to speak in other tongues as the Spirit enabled them' (vv. 3–4).

First, there was a windless hurricane, then there seemed to be fire falling from the ceiling. But instead of setting the place alight, it separated and came to rest upon each person in the room. God was making a point. The wind and the fire are both symbols of God's presence; the separating fire is a symbol of the Holy Spirit coming to live in each person. And that is exactly what happened. Each person was filled with God's presence. In the past, the Holy Spirit had only filled specific people at particular times. But now God was coming to live in each and every person who had put their trust in the resurrected Jesus. As a further sign of his presence in them, they all began speaking in other languages. These weren't the kind of tongues that you sometimes hear talked about in church, where people are able to speak in a heavenly language these were actual, earth-bound languages spoken by the people who had all gathered in Jerusalem. And what did they do with these new languages? They headed out and began 'declaring the wonders of God' (v. 11) so all the people staying in Jerusalem, from all over the known world, heard about the saving work of God in their own language.

I don't know if this reminds you of any Bible stories, but I can think of one in particular. Early in the Bible is the story of the tower of Babel (Genesis 11:1–9). The story begins when all the people on earth spoke one language, and they decided to build themselves a tower to reach the heavens, for their glory. They were attempting to leave God out of their nation-building endeavours. But as they built their tower, God decided to come down and have a look at it. It was nowhere near the necessary height to reach heaven (not to mention that heaven isn't just up; they'd have needed an inter-dimensional tower). God then confused their language so that they would no longer be able to work together, and the people were scattered all over the earth, speaking different languages.

This story is old, but it speaks about a common truth. All throughout the world we see people trying to get to God. And when they want to get to God, they go up! They build altars or temples on top of mountains, or pyramids and ziggurats. We're always reaching for God. But now, in the story of Acts, God came down. Just like in the time of Babel, he came down. This time, he came down not to judge humanity, but to bring humanity to himself. Jesus had dealt with God's judgement; now God was healing the relationship and calling people to himself. That's the point of the different languages. It's God reaching out and proclaiming the good news of heavenly peace to the people of earth – each in their own language.

It's important to notice here what the Holy Spirit compelled the disciples to do. We Christians love to talk about the Holy Spirit, some of us more than others, and there are some things that the Holy Spirit does that we get really excited about. We love the speaking in tongues thing, and the Holy Spirit healing people or giving people prophesies and words of knowledge. All these are good and important gifts from God to his people, but notice what happens when those early Christians first get the Holy Spirit. He impels them to run out into the streets and tell people about Jesus! The Holy Spirit wants people to know about Christ, and he wants us to be the ones who introduce them. We have to be careful not to get distracted by all the things we want the Holy Spirit to be doing and pay attention to what the Holy Spirit is actually asking us to do.

That said, there are other Christians who do the opposite with the Holy Spirit. We feel a bit uncomfortable with the Spirit doing crazy stuff, and we want him just to do things like help us understand the Bible, stop us from sinning, and convict people that Jesus is Lord. And of course, these are very, very important things, central to the work of the Holy Spirit. But the truth of the Spirit is that sometimes he might get the job done by weird, uncomfortable stuff happening, and that's totally fine, because the Holy Spirit is God and he can do whatever he wants.

The not-drunken speech

With the streets full of preaching disciples, the crowd began mocking the followers of Jesus because they thought they were behaving like drunk people. It was clear that someone had to do something. So Peter, who had been recently recommissioned by Jesus, stood up in front of the crowd and began to preach. The first thing he said was this: 'Fellow Jews and all of you who live in Jerusalem, let me explain this to you; listen carefully to what I say. These people are not drunk, as you suppose. It's only nine in the morning!' (Acts 2:14–15).

This was the first Christian sermon ever preached and it began with an explanation that the Christians were not drunk. Not a super auspicious beginning, is it? And what is his reason for them not being drunk? Not that they don't get drunk or haven't been drinking, just that they don't get drunk that early in the morning. 'It's only nine in the morning!' Midday maybe, three o'clock probably, 6pm for sure! But 9am? Absolutely not![65]

So if they weren't drunk, what *was* going on? Peter went on to explain. What was happening was the fulfilment of an ancient prophesy from the prophet Joel:

> In the last days, God says,
>> I will pour out my Spirit on all people.
> Your sons and daughters will prophesy,
>> your young men will see visions,
>> your old men will dream dreams.

---

65. I don't actually think the first Christians were drunks – I just think Peter's explanation is funny.

Even on my servants, both men and
women,
I will pour out my Spirit in those days,
and they will prophesy. (vv. 17–18)

God was doing a new thing, the last big thing before
he brings history to a conclusion: he has poured out his
Spirit on all people. Not just the old or the young, not
just the men or the women – all people will have access
to God, via his Spirit. Anyone can experience the power
of the Holy Spirit!

Why? Because of the work of Jesus. Peter went
on to explain it: 'Fellow Israelites, listen to this: Jesus
of Nazareth was a man accredited by God to you by
miracles, wonders and signs, which God did among
you through him, as you yourselves know. This man
was handed over to you by God's deliberate plan and
foreknowledge; and you, with the help of wicked men,
put him to death by nailing him to the cross. But God
raised him from the dead, freeing him from the agony
of death, because it was impossible for death to keep its
hold on him' (vv. 22–24). Peter was telling them that it is
because of the work of Jesus, who was sent and approved
by God, that the Holy Spirit arrived. Peter was showing
how the work of Jesus and the arrival of the Spirit were
both fulfillments of God's ancient promises. The Holy
Spirit was poured out because Jesus, the resurrected and
ascended King, is now at the right hand of God.

Then, as he came to the end of the sermon, Peter
finished with this corker:

'Therefore let all Israel be assured of this: God has made this Jesus, whom you crucified, both Lord and Messiah' (v. 36). How did the crowd respond? I can imagine everyone getting offended and deciding to stone Peter. But instead, we're told that 'they were cut to the heart and said to Peter and the other apostles, "Brothers, what shall we do?"' (v. 37). 'Peter replied, "Repent and be baptised, every one of you, in the name of Jesus Christ for the forgiveness of your sins. And you will receive the gift of the Holy Spirit. The promise is for you and your children and for all who are far off – for all whom the Lord our God will call." With many other words he warned them; and he pleaded with them, "Save yourselves from this corrupt generation." Those who accepted his message were baptised, and about three thousand were added to their number that day' (vv. 38–41).

What a start to the church of Jesus Christ! Wind and fire, people speaking in languages they've never learned, a powerful sermon, and three thousand people coming to faith in Jesus!

What interests me particularly, however, is Peter. You could be excused for not recognising the Peter that we see in this story, so different is he from the one that we have seen in all the others. Remember how Peter would say stupid things that seemed to just pop into his head? But here he was, standing and giving a theologically brilliant, off the cuff sermon for thousands of people, and he didn't say a single face-palmy thing. Remember how he once rebuked Jesus for saying he was going to die and

266

rise again? Here we find him explaining how Jesus' death and resurrection is the fulfilment of God's great plan. Remember how Peter was terrified of a young servant girl finding out that he was a follower of Jesus? Now he is standing up in front of thousands of people, telling them that they crucified the Messiah and commanding them to repent! This is a new and improved Peter that we find in Acts 2.

From this day on, things became very different. Soon after this, Peter and John were locked up for preaching to a group of people at the temple after healing a man with a disability. When they appeared before the Sanhedrin, the people who had condemned Jesus to death, Peter preached to them too, telling them, once again, that they killed Jesus and they must look to him for salvation. After this, another two thousand people became Christians (Acts 3:1—4:22).

The disciples continued to do miracles and preach about Jesus as the resurrected Lord. At one stage they were arrested by the high priest and put in jail, but an angel came and let them out. When they got out, they just kept preaching in the temple courts. When the high priest's guards managed to track them down, they brought them in to see the Sanhedrin again. When they were asked why they keep preaching even though they have been told not to, Peter, speaking for the group, said to them, 'We must obey God rather than human beings! The God of our ancestors raised Jesus from the dead – whom you killed by hanging him on a cross' (Acts 5:29–30). The disciples were then flogged and let go.

They rejoiced 'because they had been counted worthy of suffering disgrace for the Name' (Acts 5:31). This does not sound like the behaviour of the same bunch of bumblers who all ran away when Jesus was arrested.

So what is it that transforms old Peter into new Peter, the old disciples into the new disciples? How can this radical change happen overnight?

The answer is in Jesus' promise to the disciples before he left – it's the Holy Spirit! As soon as the Holy Spirit arrived at the beginning of Acts 2, all the disciples spilt out onto the streets sharing the good news of Jesus and Peter stood up and began preaching. It was the Spirit who compelled and empowered Peter and the disciples to be witnesses to the resurrection. It was the Spirit who emboldened the disciples to keep preaching even though they were persecuted, locked up, and eventually killed.

The Spirit is the secret to changing the world for Jesus. It's clear from the rest of this book that you don't have to be particularly smart, or a theological whiz, to be a giant in God's kingdom. You don't have to be a great preacher. And you certainly don't have to be sinless. The disciples were none of these things, and yet they still managed to change the world. The very fact that you are reading this book, that you know who Jesus is, is because of the disciples. If you go to church or have had any benefit from Christianity in the world (and I assure you, you have), it is because the disciples changed the world. They did it through the power of God living in them by the Holy Spirit, giving them exactly what they needed to share the good news of Jesus with the world. The people they told also received the Spirit and passed on the good news. The people they told received the Spirit too, and they shared the gospel with others. And on, and on, and on, for thousands of years, to today, where you and I are both recipients of the life-changing, universe-shifting, heaven and earth-recreating good news of Jesus Christ, who lived, died, rose, and is coming back again.

You, the world changer

So how are you feeling about all this? Excited? Intimidated? Empowered? Overwhelmed?

Perhaps you feel the pressure to be a mega-Christian, just like the disciples, and seeing as you have the Holy Spirit, you should go out and change the world too!

Please don't feel that pressure. This is not what this book is about. I hope you and I have been honest enough with each other and ourselves to admit that neither of us are mega-Christians (okay, you may be one, but I definitely am not). What I want you to see is that just as you are like the disciples – in your mistakes, your ill-timed words, your misplaced rebukes, your violent outbursts (have you cut anyone's ear off lately?), your faithlessness and your fear, your timidity, and your inability to get things right – you are at no more of a disadvantage than any of Jesus' first followers were. In fact, your mistakes and sins put you in good company with every one of Jesus' followers. But just like the disciples, you have access to the same power that they had. The promise of the Bible is that if you are in Christ, you have the Holy Spirit living in you (Romans 8:9–11).

269

You don't have to be held back by your weaknesses. In fact, your weakness is a great opportunity for God to show his strength. That is why the apostle Paul (who wrote about a third of the New Testament) writes in 2 Corinthians, 'I will boast all the more gladly about my weaknesses, so that Christ's power may rest on me. That is why, for Christ's sake, I delight in weaknesses, in insults, in hardships, in persecutions, in difficulties. For when I am weak, then I am strong' (2 Corinthians 12:9–10). Your weakness is not a reason to give up. It's a reason to press on so that you can see how strong you can be when God works through you. You don't have to change the world, that's already happened. But you do get to change *your* world. You do this by choosing to follow Jesus wherever he leads you, to love the people he puts before you, to be brave enough to share the good news of what he has done, and to tell the stories of how you have seen the resurrected Jesus at work in your life. You may not be any more impressive than anyone else, but if you entrust your work to the power of the Holy Spirit, you will see people come to faith in Jesus, and you will see people grow in their love for Jesus.

'Okay, that all sounds amazing! But what do I actually do to get the Holy Spirit?'

The great news is you don't have to do any kind of hocus pocus. You don't have to perform any special ritual or have someone holy pray for you, nor do you have to have flames fall on your head or speak in a different language. If you trust in Jesus as your risen Saviour, who by his death and resurrection has saved you from the just penalty for your sin and welcomed you into his family, then you have the Holy Spirit. You don't even need to do anything to 'activate' the Spirit. In some ways this is easier than getting an account on any website, because you don't even need to verify your email address. The Holy Spirit is already at work in you. There may be times when you experience the presence of the Holy Spirit in a special way, but that doesn't make him any less at work when you're not feeling it. He is living in you – you can trust him to work.

My experience is this: if you're willing to take the first step of obedience, no matter how scared you are, God will turn up. Just pray and ask for God's help, then do whatever it is you need to do, and you'll get to see what God does through your obedience. Sometimes you may feel confident, like the Holy Spirit is in you empowering you, other times you might feel weak and scared, but either way, he'll turn up.

I was employed to be a youth minister at a church on Sydney's Northern Beaches at the ripe old age of nineteen. I had one year's experience working as the student youth worker at the church I grew up in, and that was it. I had pimples on my face, terrible clothes, and the distinct feeling of being a failure. In my previous role, when I was still only eighteen, I had achieved a lot less than I had hoped. The youth group had shrunk, the church service I led had shut down, and I wasn't really sure if I had achieved anything.

Now I'm thirty-eight years old, and I'm still working as youth minister, for a group of churches in Melbourne's inner north. I am a lot more experienced than in those early years. I have a degree under my belt, another one on the way, and I've done thousands of hours of ministry, working in a few different roles in churches and in Christian organisations. I've sold thousands of books and spoken to many thousands more people about Jesus.[66] And I'll tell you what – I feel a lot more like that nineteen-year-old than I care to admit. I still feel like I have no idea what I'm doing. I regularly think about how to lead this ministry, and all I can do is pray and say, 'God, I have no idea what I'm doing. Please do your thing.' As I sit here writing, I'm still not sure if this book is any good. I'm right at the very end, and I think it might just be a bunch of words.

But let me tell you something that I have seen during my time in ministry and as a follower of Jesus. God turns up. I have seen young people come to know Jesus. I have seen people find a new community who love them and care for them in the church. I have seen young people step into ministry themselves. I have seen people get healed, and I have seen many people become more like Jesus. And I have been able to play a part in those things. Not because I'm a super-Christian (I hope by now my bona fides as being mediocre at best have been established), but because the Holy Spirit works through his people, and I am one of them.

There's an adventure waiting for you. There is work to be done. There are words to be spoken, prayers to

---

66. When I say I've sold thousands of books, let me be clear, the number is in the low thousands. I'm not a big deal.

be prayed, people to be loved, lives to be changed, and good news to be shared. If you step out in faith, obedient to what Jesus is calling you to, I promise the Holy Spirit will get to work through you. Why? Because he wants people to know Jesus even more than you do, he's more invested in growing his kingdom than you are, and he loves the people you meet more than you ever can. With the Holy Spirit, you can change your world – and maybe, just maybe, he'll use you to change the whole world.

CONCLUSION

The Further Adventures of the Disciples

Congratulations on making it to the end of the book! Now you can go and put it on your bookcase, take it off your reading pile, mark it as finished, or add it to your Goodreads list. Goodreads is where it's at for me. I reckon I finish about fifty per cent of the books that I start just so I can meet my reading challenge and impress all those people who like to follow my reading challenge (read: no one).

Gosh, what a dull way to start a conclusion.

I know I had that rousing ending in the final chapter, but I suspect some of you are sitting there wondering, 'What happened to the disciples afterwards? Did they just stop doing stupid stuff?' So I figure we should cover that before I let you put this book on your shelf or leave it on your e-reader.

What *did* happen to the disciples?

Well they certainly didn't stop doing daft things. Although there aren't nearly as many stories after Acts 2 about the not-so-smart stuff they did, we do know a bit about what Peter got up to.

There's an excellent story in Acts 10 when Peter went up to a roof at lunchtime to pray. But it was lunchtime, and he was hungry, so he got distracted by a vision of food. Specifically, he had a vision from God of a big sheet of animals, some of which were ceremonially unclean for a Jew to eat, being let down from the sky. Then the voice of God told him, 'Get up, Peter. Kill and eat!'

Peter replied, 'Surely not, Lord! I have never eaten anything impure or unclean.'

To which God replied, 'Do not call anything impure that God has made clean' (Acts 10:13–15).

This same conversation happened three times, exactly the same way. Poor old Peter. He just can't say the right thing. He tells God he can't eat because he won't eat unclean food, which you think would be the right thing to do, and then he gets in trouble for it! He just can't win.[67]

The point of all this was not to teach Peter that he was now allowed to eat bacon (Jesus had already made that point in Mark 7:18–19, which is also the only place where Jesus makes a poo joke), but to teach him that no person that God has made is unclean. While the Jews would only associate with the Jews, God wanted Peter and the other disciples to bring the good news of Jesus to everyone – Jew or not.

---

67. I remember the Texan pastor, Matt Chandler, pointing this out in a sermon I was listening to online, and I laughed out loud. I have pointed it out in talks I've given on this passage since then and it only ever receives a small 'Ha'. I assume this is because a) Matt Chandler is funnier than me, and b) I did a bad job at stealing his joke.

It seems a bit odd that Peter had to be told this, because Jesus seemed to have made this clear, too, when he told the disciples to be his witnesses in 'Jerusalem, and in all Judea and Samaria, and to the ends of the earth' (Acts 1:8).

Still, Peter got the point eventually. He started telling Gentiles (people who weren't Jewish) about Jesus, and baptising them. This upset the other disciples, so he had to explain his actions. After he told them what happened with the dream and the command to share the gospel with non-Jews, they all thought it was a great idea, but may I remind you that Jesus had already given them the idea when he told them to be his witnesses in 'Jerusalem, and in all Judea and Samaria, and to the ends of the earth'!

But alas! Even though Peter was the one who brought the message of Gentile acceptance and cleanliness to the new Christian church, he slipped back into his old ways. The apostle Paul writes in Galatians about how he had to rebuke Peter because he had stopped eating with Gentiles and was treating them like second-class citizens again (Galatians 2:11–14). That must have been one of the great theological battles of history.

So from what we can see in the Bible, the disciples didn't just get the Holy Spirit and were suddenly perfect. (Apologies if this bursts your bubble. If the holy apostles didn't reach a state of sinlessness, you're not going to either, at least not till you meet Jesus in the flesh.) But they were permanently changed and ended up being anything but disappointing. Together, they went on to share the good news of Jesus in 'Jerusalem, and in all Judea and Samaria, and to the ends of the earth.' All the disciples were willing to suffer for their faith in Jesus (Act 5:17–42). They all remained faithful in witnessing to the resurrection of Jesus until their deaths. While the Bible only tells us about the death of James, we have some church traditions and ancient documents that give us a picture of how the other disciples died. Many were martyred – killed because of their faithful witnessing to the lordship of Jesus. Not all the accounts of their deaths may be entirely accurate, but from everything we know, they were faithful to the end.

Here's a quick overview of the deaths of the apostles:[68]

Simon Peter

Peter, as he was now known, is said to have gone to Rome to preach and lead the church there. He was most likely executed under the persecution of the Emperor Nero between AD 64 and 67. In all likelihood, he was crucified – making sense of Jesus' prophecy about his death in John 21:18–19. Tradition says that he asked to

---

68. I have drawn most of my information on the deaths of the apostles from Sean McDowell's book *The Fate of the Apostles*. The book seeks to establish how reliable various sources are relating to the accounts of the martyrdom of each apostle. Some things are more likely than others, but I've done my best to let you know what seems possible. There are a lot more great stories out there, so feel free to read Dr McDowell's book to get all the juicy tales. Sean McDowell, *The Fate of the Apostles: Examining the Martyrdom Accounts of the Closest Followers of Jesus* (Abingdon: Routledge, 2016).

be crucified upside down as he didn't feel worthy to be crucified in the same manner as his Lord.

James

James, the brother of John, was the first of the apostles to be martyred for his faith. We read about this in Acts 12:1–3: 'It was about this time that King Herod arrested some who belonged to the church, intending to persecute them. He had James, the brother of John, put to death with the sword. When he saw that this met with approval among the Jews, he proceeded to seize Peter also.'

The one who wanted to sit on a throne beside Jesus, did indeed drink the cup Jesus drank, and was baptised with the baptism Jesus was baptised with (Mark 10:39). The same Herod who allowed Jesus to be put to death had James put to death. James found greatness. Not the greatness he was looking for, but a greater greatness in his faithfulness to his Lord.

John

We don't know exactly how John died. We do know that, compared to the other apostles, he lived a long life. He is believed to have written the Gospel of John, as well as the letters 1, 2, and 3 John, and the book of Revelation. John is believed to have received the visions of the book of Revelation, which encourages the church to remain faithful to Jesus even in the face of terrible persecution, while he was exiled on Patmos (a small Greek island off the coast of Turkey). Later, it is thought that he led the church in Ephesus (the same church Paul wrote the book of Ephesians to), where he died an old man.

Andrew

Andrew, Peter's brother, who we saw in the Gospel of John bringing people to Jesus, most likely continued to do just that. Some ancient accounts have him travelling to Greece to share the good news of Jesus there. There is a story that says he was crucified on a cross, but without nails. As he hung from the cross, he preached for four days before he died. This may just be a good story, but there is no reason to think that he wasn't killed for his faith.

Philip

Philip is thought to have travelled as an evangelist, settling in the city of Hierapolis, where he died. There are some traditions that say he was martyred there. There is even one story about Philip being crucified upside down for condemning idol worship. When he was on the cross, he cursed the crowd and the earth opened up and swallowed the people, their temple, and their god, killing 8,000 people. Jesus then turned up and told Philip off. This wild story is very unlikely to be true, but that doesn't mean he didn't die for his faith – it just means we don't really know much about his death.

Bartholomew

Given the last two stories, you may be hoping for an even more impressive story about Bartholomew. There are stories of Bartholomew travelling to, and being martyred in, three different countries. In Parthia (which is around modern-day Iran), he is said to have angered the king with his preaching, so he was thrown into the sea in a sack full of sand. In Armenia, he is said to have been crucified upside down. In India, he is said to have been beaten with clubs and then beheaded by priests. There is no reason to believe that he died all these deaths (that would be very strange), but at the very least, all the traditions have him being killed for his faithful preaching of the gospel to people who needed Jesus.

Matthew

There are so many different stories about what Matthew did after Jesus' ascension, I won't list them here. Apart from writing the Gospel of Matthew, there is very little consensus. There are, however, many stories of all sorts of different ways that he was martyred. Whatever happened, it's very likely he was faithful to Jesus to the very end.

Thomas

Thomas, who once doubted, most likely went to India to preach the gospel, where he was killed for his witness to Jesus. Tradition says that he was speared to death.

James son of Alphaeus

There isn't much information about James. There are a few stories that say he was martyred, but none are particularly conclusive. We know little about him in the

Bible, and we know little about him after the Bible, but in all the stories we have he was either stoned to death or crucified because of his commitment to his Lord.

Thaddaeus

Like most of these minor apostles (hey, even being a minor apostle is a big deal!), we know about as much about Thaddeus after Jesus' ascension as before. That is to say, almost nothing. There are lots of stories, but none are conclusive. He may have been martyred, or he may have lived till old age. From everything we know, however, he preached the good news of Jesus faithfully till the end.

Simon the Zealot

I don't want to keep repeating myself, but we know next to nothing about what happened to Simon the Zealot. Some people think he went to Britain and preached there. He may also have invented bubble and squeak. What we do know is he was commissioned by Jesus, with the others, to take the gospel to the ends of the earth, and we can safely assume that that is what he did.

Mathias

Remember Mathias? He was the guy who replaced Judas after he died, and then we never saw him in the Bible again (Acts 1:12–26). Well, we don't know much about his death either. But seeing as he was willing to suffer for the sake of proclaiming Jesus with the other apostles, we can trust that he continued to do that till his final day.

* * *

It's clear from the lives of the disciples, no matter how much or how little we know about them, that following Jesus doesn't promise to be fun or easy. But just as the Holy Spirit transformed them, enabling them to be faithful even to the point of death, he will also empower you to live a faithful life. What is Jesus calling you to? Don't sell yourself short. Don't dream small.

Jesus is calling you to follow him, and it will cost you everything you have. Your ambitions, your time, your money, and more. You probably won't find fame or fortune, but you will find an adventure with Jesus. He'll send you places you never dreamed you could or would go. He'll call you to love people you never thought you could love. You may be scared because you don't think you can do it, but you can and you will. You don't go alone. You go with the Holy Spirit in you, and with the people of Jesus by your side. You can achieve what you never thought you could achieve, because you have God in you, beside you, before you, and behind you. You have everything you need. If the first disciples could do it, you can too. Go for it!

WHAT'S NEXT?

To receive a free book and updates on Tom's latest news and new releases, head to:

tomfrench.com.au/freebook

FURTHER READING

Writing a book takes a lot of work. I don't have a lot of natural knowledge of the Bible myself so I need a lot of help from people smarter and with more expertise than me. So here is a list of the books that I specifically referred to in my preparation. If you were to read them, you'd see that most of my thoughts are not original. Happily I made up most of the jokes myself; almost none of them are in these books. If you want to know more about Jesus, his disciples, and the Bible in general, dive in. These books will give you a lot more to think about.

Augsburger, Myron. *Matthew*. Vol. 24. The Preacher's Commentary. Nashville: Thomas Nelson, 2002.

Barclay, William. *The Gospel of John, Volume One–Chapters 1 to 7*. Edinburgh: Saint Andrew Press, 1975.

Blomberg, Craig L. *Matthew*. The New American Commentary, v. 22. Nashville: Broadman, 1992.

Bock, Darrell L. *Luke*. The NIV Application Commentary Series. Grand Rapids: Zondervan, 1996.

Borchert, Gerald L. *John 1–11*. Vol. 25A. The New American Commentary. Nashville: Broadman & Holman, 1996.

Borchert, Gerald L. *John 12–21*. Vol. 25B. The New American Commentary. Nashville: Broadman & Holman, 2002.

Brooks, James A. *Mark*. Nashville: Broadman, 1991.

Bruce, F. F. *The Gospel of John*. Grand Rapids: Eerdmans, 1994.

Burge, Gary M. *John*. The NIV Application Commentary. Grand Rapids: Zondervan, 2000.

Carson, D. A. *The Gospel According to John*. Grand Rapids: Eerdmans, 1991.

Carson, D. A. *Matthew*. The Expositor's Bible Commentary Revised Series 9. Grand Rapids: Zondervan, 2010.

Edwards, James R. *The Gospel According to Mark*. The Pillar New Testament Commentary. Grand Rapids: Eerdmans; Leicester: Apollos, 2002.

English, Donald. *The Message of Mark*. The Bible Speaks Today. Leicester: Inter-Varsity Press, 1992.

Evans, Craig A. and Porter, Stanley, E. eds. *Dictionary of New Testament Background*. Downers Grove: IVP Academic, 2000.

Fernando, Ajith. *Acts*. The NIV Application Commentary. Grand Rapids: Zondervan, 1998.

France, R. T. *The Gospel of Mark: A Commentary on the Greek Text*. The New International Greek Testament Commentary. Grand Rapids: Eerdmans; Carlisle: Paternoster, 2002.

France, R. T. *The Gospel of Matthew*. The New International Commentary on the New Testament. Grand Rapids: Eerdmans, 2007.

Fredrikson, Roger L. *John*. Vol. 27. The Preacher's Commentary. Nashville: Thomas Nelson, 1985.

Gaebelein, Frank Ely, ed. *Matthew, Mark, Luke*. The Expositor's Bible Commentary. Vol. 8. Grand Rapids: Zondervan, 1984.

Garland, David E. *Mark*. The NIV Application Commentary. Grand Rapids: Zondervan, 1996.

Green, Joel B. *The Gospel of Luke*. The New International Commentary on the New Testament. Grand Rapids: Eerdmans, 1997.

Green, Joel B., ed. *Dictionary of Jesus and the Gospels*. Second Edition. Downers Grove: IVP Academic, 2013.

Hochhalter, Daniel. *Losers Like Us: Redefining Discipleship after Epic Failure*. Colorado Springs: David C Cook, 2014.

Keller, Timothy. *King's Cross: The Story of the World in the Life of Jesus*. London: Hodder & Stoughton, 2013.

Larson, Bruce. *Luke*. Vol. 26. The Preacher's Commentary. Nashville: Thomas Nelson, 2003.

MacArthur, John. *Twelve Ordinary Men: How the Master Shaped His Disciples for Greatness, and What He Wants to Do with You*. Nashville: Thomas Nelson, 2006.

McDowell, Sean. *The Fate of the Apostles: Examining the Martyrdom Accounts of the Closest Followers of Jesus*. Abingdon: Routledge, 2016.

McKenna, David L. *Mark*. Vol. 25. The Preacher's Commentary. Nashville: Thomas Nelson, 2003.

McKinley, Mike. *Luke 1–12 For You*. Epsom: The Good Book Company, 2016.

McKinley, Mike. *Luke 12–24 For You*. Epsom: The Good Book Company, 2017.

Milne, Bruce. *The Message of John*. The Bible Speaks Today. Leicester: Inter-Varsity Press, 1993.

Moody, Josh. *John 1–12 For You*. Epsom: The Good Book Company, 2017.

Moody, Josh. *John 13–21 For You*. Epsom: The Good Book Company, 2019.

Morris, Leon. *The Gospel According to Matthew*. The New International Commentary on the New Testament. Grand Rapids: Eerdmans , 1992.

Morris, Leon. *The Gospel According to John*. Rev. ed. The New International Commentary on the New Testament. Grand Rapids: Eerdmans, 2008.

Ogilvie, Lloyd John. *Acts*. Vol. 28. The Preacher's Commentary. Nashville: Thomas Nelson, 2010.

Polhill, John B. *Acts*. Vol. 26. The New American Commentary. Nashville: Broadman, 1992.

Stein, Robert H. *Luke*. Vol. 24. The New American Commentary. Nashville: Broadman, 1992.

Wilcock, Michael. *The Message of Luke*. The Bible Speaks Today. Nottingham: Inter-Varsity Press, 1979.

Wilkins, Michael J. *Matthew*. The NIV Application Commentary. Grand Rapids: Zondervan, 2004.

Wright, N. T. *Luke for Everyone*. 2nd ed. London: SPCK; Louisville: Westminster John Knox Press, 2004.

ALSO BY TOM FRENCH

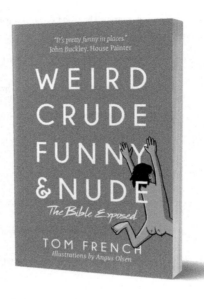

'Grab this book with both hands and see where it takes you!'
Ali Martin, Soul Survivor UK

Ultimate fighting bears, a fat king who poops himself, zombies, donkey 'bits', and a fart.

These are not the things you'd expect to find in the Bible, but they're all there. If you thought the Bible was dull, think again. This is your chance to discover all the parts of the Bible they don't teach you in Sunday school – but probably should.

Weird, Crude, Funny, and Nude is a hilarious, Christ-centred, and somewhat inappropriate look at some of the least known and discussed parts of the Bible – perfect for teenagers or any of us who think nudity, poop, and farts are funny.

BUY NOW AT TOMFRENCH.COM.AU

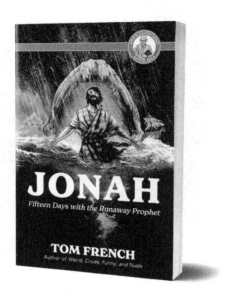

Do you ever feel less than heroic in your faith?

Jonah is the prophet for you. He's a scared, overly-emotional, responsibility-avoiding, anti-hero of biblical proportions. As you struggle with how to respond to your calling, how to treat your enemies, your disappointment with God, and how to escape the belly of a giant fish, these devotions with Jonah will challenge, encourage, and delight you.

Pop's Devotions is a series of engaging daily devotions, written for young people, that works through books of the Bible from beginning to end.

BUY NOW AT TOMFRENCH.COM.AU

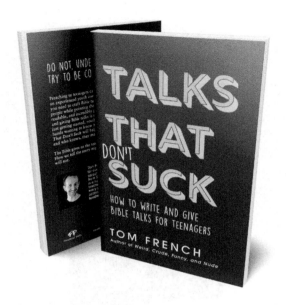

'Do not, under any circumstances, try to be cooler than you are.'

Preaching to teenagers can be a terrifying prospect. Tom French, an experienced youth communicator, will give you everything you need to craft Bible talks that engage and challenge young people while pointing them to the love of God in Jesus. This fun, readable, and incredibly practical step-by-step guide for writing and giving Bible talks is the ideal book for new youth leaders just getting started, youth pastors looking for a refresher, or old hands wanting to know how to speak to young people. *Talks That Don't Suck* will help you ensure your talks aren't terrible –and who knows, they may even be amazing!

The Bible gives us the story for all people, for all generations. How we tell the story might change, but the truth of the story will not.

ABOUT THE AUTHOR

Tom French is married to his excellent wife, Emily Sandrussi. He is also a youth ministry veteran, having spent the past two decades working with teenagers in churches and schools around Australia. Every year he teaches the Bible to thousands of young people in youth groups, churches, schools, and camps around the country. He has a Bachelor of Theology from Sydney Missionary and Bible College.

Tom lives in Melbourne with Emily and their daughter, Layla. You can often find him on his couch eating popcorn for dinner.

Visit **tomfrench.com.au** to receive a free ebook, blog updates, and the latest on new books. There you can also listen to Tom's sermons, book Tom to speak, see a photo of Tom holding a microphone, and much more.

YouTube: **youtube.com/twfrench**
Instagram: **@twfrench**
Facebook: **facebook.com/twfrench**

Podcast: Search for **'Tom French Preaching'** in your favourite podcast app

Made in the USA
Las Vegas, NV
05 January 2022

40518960R00164